ENDORSEMENTS

"Powerful and deeply wise, Olivia Hoblitzelle's *Aging with Wisdom* meets a growing cultural need: new ways to relate to aging. Olivia sheds light on a skillful relationship with aging by sharing from her own experience and by turning back toward the teachings of the Buddha. This is a wonderful book, much needed, and I highly recommend it to mature and young readers alike." —SHARON SALZBERG, AUTHOR OF *Lovingkindness* and *Real Happiness*

"This book is like a multi-colored jeweled necklace, each brief chapter distinctive in its brilliance, wisdom, and heart-moving content. It is honest about the tribulations of aging while inspiring each of us to find meaning as we move toward death and the light. Olivia's stories and perspective are so exquisitely written; you will find yourself in tears and laughter, bringing you to face your own journey of aging in new ways." —NATALIE ROGERS, AUTHOR OF *The Creative Connection: Expressive Arts As Healing*

"Caution! Do not attempt to read this book rapidly. It is essential to pause and ponder after each brief reflection. For Olivia Hoblitzelle is a rare person and this is a rare book. The reader will be rewarded with a new paradigm of aging. . . . A gem to be treasured!" —RABBI EARL GROLLMAN, AUTHOR OF 27 BOOKS INCLUDING *Living When a Loved One Has Died*

"Inviting and encouraging, *Aging with Wisdom* offers great inspiration to all those who would like to use their later years to ripen spiritually, to awaken." —KATHLEEN DOWLING SINGH, AUTHOR OF *The Grace in Aging, The Grace in Dying*

"Once again Olivia generously shares with us her wise woman and spiritual elder perspectives on aging and sageing, with grace and wonder, loving-kindness, patience and humility. Her unequalled passion for exploring and cultivating the positive opportunities of aging without turning away from the gritty and painful parts of the process is an instructive inspiration to us all, an awakened vision which can transform our later years. These are timeless and timely life lessons opening to the great mystery of existence, of love, and of being alone yet connected here together through birth, death, and onwards."
—LAMA SURYA DAS, FOUNDER OF THE DZOGCHEN MEDITATION CENTER AND DZOGCHEN RETREATS, AND AUTHOR OF *Awakening the Buddha Within: Tibetan Wisdom for the Western World*

"Drawing deeply on her own experiences as well as stories and studies about aging from other cultures, Hoblitzelle (*Ten Thousand Joys & Ten Thousand Sorrows*) explores the ways that readers can nourish their inner lives and spirit even as their bodies age and facilities diminish. Hoblitzelle stresses the reflective nature of the aging process: noticing how the body changes can provide space for reflection on life's gifts and challenges, and aging often brings family members together, creating an opportunity to heal broken relationships. She offers seven guidelines to being attentive to the gifts that grow more valuable with age: spiritual orientation, practice of silence, practice of mindfulness, practice of stopping, finding the sacred in the commonplace, meditation, and the practice of gratitude. She also shares the stories of six 'wayshowers,' individuals whose stories illustrate aging with compassion (Emerson Stamps reflects on his enslaved African ancestors while writing a memoir in his 80s, and Maud Morgan finds solace in the words of Jesuit priest Pierre Teilhard de Chardin: 'The world is filled and filled with the absolute—to see this is to be free'). Hoblitzelle's heartfelt book invites inspiring reflections on finding beauty in aging, facing death with dignity, and rejoicing in earthly blessings." —*Publishers Weekly*

AGING
with
WISDOM

AGING
with
WISDOM

REFLECTIONS, STORIES
AND TEACHINGS

Olivia Ames Hoblitzelle

Monkfish Book Publishing Company
Rhinebeck, New York

Aging with Wisdom: Reflections, Stories and Teachings © 2017 by Olivia Ames Hoblitzelle

Cover design by Nita Ybarra
Book design by Colin Rolfe

Paperback ISBN: 978-1-939681-71-3
eBook ISBN: 978-1-939681-72-0

Library of Congress Cataloging-in-Publication Data

Names: Hoblitzelle, Olivia Ames, author.
Title: Aging with wisdom : reflections, stories and teachings / Olivia Ames Hoblitzelle.
Description: Rhinebeck, New York : Monkfish Book Publishing Company, [2017] | Includes bibliographical references.
Identifiers: LCCN 2017027120 (print) | LCCN 2017008600 (ebook) | ISBN 9781939681713 (pbk. : alk. paper) | ISBN 9781939681720 (ebook)
Subjects: LCSH: Spiritual life--Buddhism. | Old age--Religious aspects--Buddhism.
Classification: LCC BQ5660 .H63 2017 (ebook) | LCC BQ5660 (print) | DDC 294.3/4440846--dc23
LC record available at https://lccn.loc.gov/2017027120

Monkfish Book Publishing Company
22 East Market Street, Suite 304
Rhinebeck, New York 12572
USA (845) 876-4861
www.monkfishpublishing.com

To my parents and grandparents with deep gatitude,
and in honor of all elders everywhere.

TABLE OF CONTENTS

Foreword

DEAR READERS, YOU are in very good hands. You are about to start this beautifully written and profound book that can take you deeply into self-discovery—if you let it!

But first, a bit about my own point of view. I have spent about forty years as a student, practitioner, and teacher of Buddhism. These years include a focus on aging, sickness, and death, considered central to the Buddha. I have received a great deal of specialized meditation training in this area, have read much Buddhist writing about it, and have even written a book on this subject.

For the Buddha, learning how to live and learning how to die are inseparable. I am happy to be invited to write this foreword on such a vital subject. A full reading of the manuscript reveals a fresh and unique approach, one that has the potential to help bring the reader into intimacy with what we all face: aging, illness, and death. Olivia has put together a medley of sincere personal reflections, poetry, scriptures from different spiritual traditions, and insights of ancient and contemporary sages.

It is a book about wisdom and compassion. The same? Different? Wisdom without compassion can be cold; compassion without wisdom even dangerous. I suggest that you read these wisdom teachings with an open heart. Let the words reveal the energy that is inside them and let these words work on you.

As we age, grow ill, and face death, are we suffering more than we need to? Wisdom is the insightful seeing and understanding that enables us to face joy and sorrow—and go beyond both. For me, this collection of writings is a Yogic Manual: words designed to help awaken the wisdom that lies dormant in each and every one of us. Dear reader, you are in very good hands, indeed.

–Larry Rosenberg
Founder and Guiding Teacher, Cambridge Insight Meditation Center
Author, *Three Steps to Awakening: A Practice for Bringing Mindfulness to Life*
Cambridge, MA
March, 2017

INTRODUCTION

MUCH OF LIFE comes down to a matter of perspective. Given this truth, how do perspectives change for elders and how do we handle the process of our aging? Each of us will have our own answers, but speaking generally, the elder years ask for another kind of growth, different from our earlier years. They invite continuing discovery, deepening the inner life, and opening to the mystery in which we live.

Now in my late seventies, I live with persistent questions about what it's like to be an elder in a culture that, for the most part, doesn't respect its elders. Not only that, but a culture that shies away from the realities of old age, death, and dying. Yet these are the realities that give great depth and richness to life.

Questions and challenges abound: How do we find beauty and meaning in old age? How do we overturn the paradigm of age-ism? How do we age consciously and cultivate an inner life that is resilient enough to withstand the vicissitudes of old age?

Aging with Wisdom reflects on these questions. As I was called to write about this subject, I began to regard these musings as a kind of memoir of my seventies—an extended meditation on how to age consciously and embrace life in all its fullness and wonder. I was not only living with these questions, but I realized that something significant had shifted in my life. I watched as friends received serious medical diagnoses. I accompanied them to doctor's appointments as their advocate, stood by them as they dealt with life-threatening illnesses, and eventually sat vigil as they moved toward death. This new dimension of life had quietly insinuated itself into the relative complacency of my middle years when old age and death still seemed like distant prospects.

Reflecting on this new perspective, I'm reminded of an enduring legend from the Buddhist tradition. Previously I had seen it as a colorful story, but now its deeper meaning demanded attention. As the story goes, Prince Siddhartha, later to become the Buddha, lived a protected life in the palace and extensive gardens of his father. At age twenty-nine, the prince became restless and curious about what lay outside the royal realm. He ventured forth from the palace, and there he saw, in succession, an old man, a sick man, a corpse, and a wandering contemplative. These were called "the four heavenly messengers," sent by the gods to alter the course of his life. Because the king had forced a sheltered life upon his son, Siddhartha was shocked to encounter these challenging sights. *Was this the inevitable trajectory of all lives?* he asked himself.

When Siddhartha beheld the serene expression of the wandering monk, he saw a path he wanted to take where even old age, sickness, and death could be transcended through contemplation. The message of the story is that there are dimensions beyond aging, sickness, and death—that ultimate freedom is possible.

After his encounter with the four heavenly messengers, Siddhartha left the palace, dedicated his life to contemplative practice, and became enlightened; thereafter, he was called the Buddha—the awakened one.

Why are the harsh realities of the story called heavenly messengers? When we wake up to the inevitability of our own diminishment and death, we realize how precious and transient our lives are. This is a wake-up call for all of us. Some may start exploring philosophy or religion; others may feel a sense of urgency, a longing to be free from the apparent meaninglessness of old age, sickness, and death. Is that possible, you might ask?

This legend echoes our own lives. We coast along with relative well-being, preoccupied and distracted by the complexities of our lives, oblivious to what lies ahead, until one day when we are shocked with the news of a serious illness. Suddenly we're in a new reality for which we can never quite be prepared.

Aging with Wisdom is a collection of reflections, stories, and what I call wisdom treasures—thought-provoking vignettes that have inspired me during this phase of life. My assumption is that, with the inevitable diminishments of age, the inner life calls. The more resilient our spiritual life—whatever form it takes—the greater our inner resources for handling whatever comes our way. The elder stage of life is a time for consolidating, reflecting, and diving deeply into the realms of spirit we may or may not have had the time or inclination to pursue until now.

Of the many influences that illumine these pages, let me mention the key ones. As a child, I was curious about the mysteries of life and perplexed that the people around me didn't talk about these things. Who am I really? Why do I feel separate from others? What happened to my pets when they died? What about those billions of stars in the night sky? And on and on. My existential questions persisted and led to a lifetime of searching, teaching, and being a friend and student of wise elders. Typical of the exploring of the 1960s and '70s, I practiced in several spiritual traditions and ended up with a longtime Buddhist practice. Not surprisingly, this book is informed by perspectives from Buddhism as well as from other wisdom traditions.

Another influence came through my husband Harrison, known as Hob, who appears in the book. As lifelong seekers, our lives overlapped in uncanny ways: we both worked in the field of psychology and also shared Buddhist practice and teaching. Because of our backgrounds, when Hob was diagnosed with Alzheimer's, we were able to bring the wisdom of our training to negotiate his heartbreaking illness. Given our particular perspectives and inspired by the remarkable way he handled his illness, I wrote about our journey in *Ten Thousand Joys & Ten Thousand Sorrows: A Couple's Journey Through Alzheimer's.*

Not knowing what challenges lie ahead as we age, we need some form of faith or practice, ways of being with the mind and heart that we can rely on for inspiration and support. We need equanimity, resilience, and courage—all cultivated by a practice and a life continuing to be fully lived.

As I've come to see it, the last chapter of life is the most heroic. That's a powerful reframing of the current paradigm. Elders are invariably hit with a cascade of challenges, yet how they live through their late years can become an inspiration and teaching for others. Above all, *Aging with Wisdom* invites you, dear reader, to share in this journey of exploring the mysteries, wonders, and challenges of growing older. May we ripen in wisdom for the benefit of all whose lives we touch.

PART I

AGING:
REFLECTIONS, STORIES, AND MYSTERIES

The Tectonic Shift

No one knows when it happens, or even exactly how, but somewhere in the late middle years, at a different time and in different ways for each of us, a deep shift takes place within the psyche, like the shifting of tectonic plates beneath the earth's surface. It is propelled by some mysterious combination of our life experience, how we have negotiated life's challenges, the body's inevitable decline, and, above all, by our search for meaning through the different phases of our life.

What is shifting? From what to what? It's easy to identify the qualities of the energy that characterized our earlier years: the search for a career, a partner, creative expression, our place in the order of things, all propelled by a combination of calling and ambition and a wish to do well whatever our chosen path. There may still be competitiveness, or comparisons to others, or doubts about career choices and whether they honor our gifts. The thrust of expectations may be our own or those internalized from parents, heritage, or culture in general. However it was in your particular case, life in early adulthood is governed by ego, a necessity for negotiating the world, but which may become too rigid and fixed a frame of reference as our later years unfold. No longer is there the urgency to prove ourselves or control so many aspects of life. This is a pivotal shift in life's journey.

The ego—the personal "I" as distinguished from essential Self—is the navigator in early and middle adulthood, the one at the wheel, charting life's course, managing the whole *mishegas*, the craziness of living in today's Western culture—making a living, raising a family, house holding, paying bills, keeping the body together, responding to the endless cascade of information and demands coming from our i-This and our i-That, email, and media.

This shift begins imperceptibly as the body begins to talk back to us with its aches and pains, when eyesight and hearing start to diminish, when our job doesn't seem to hold the brightness that it once did, when the kids—if we had them—seem to have launched themselves (even if they return to the nest during perplexing interludes), when the myriad demands of our outer lives begin to feel more burdensome and less satisfying, when we begin to feel a softer, gentler rhythm calling from deep within us.

The bright, brilliant, sometimes rough outer edges of the earlier years—the ego riding high and propelling us along—seem to have mellowed. Instead of climbing the mountain of daily demands, a gentler landscape appears, bringing relief from the fire and urgency of earlier years. The fire has burned down to a more steady, balanced flame—still a flame, still dynamic, but no longer with the insistence of youth.

Unless you have reached this stage and experienced this shift, you cannot understand what your elders are talking about. You might puzzle over it, or even deplore it. "That's not going to happen to me," you might protest, but you know not whereof you speak. And so it should be. You are still in the vibrant, outgoing, establishing, accomplishing, proving phase of your life.

Praise be for the tectonic shift that leads us into the later stages of life where other voices are calling, the pace is different, and new horizons beckon that are equally compelling. These voices will take forms unique to each person, but they include a universal invitation: to slow to a gentler pace, to simplify, to savor the mystery of life. The reality of death is now closer, and we don't know how much time we have to harvest the fruit of our lives, look back over the many paths traveled and integrate all that we have sown and reaped. Because some form of life review is a common impulse for elders, we may wish to share the memorable moments of our lives with family and friends through writing, recording, or videoing our stories. Above all, we need to let the balance shift from the extroverted, busy, productive, "doing" phases of life toward more interiority, the more introverted, quiet, reflective, contemplative, "being" phase of life.

Some recognize that this is the time of life for "soul work," a time to reflect on the gifts, challenges, joys, and sorrows of life, to come to a sense of resolution and wholeness, particularly with what has been disappointing, disillusioning, or traumatic. This is the time to heal broken relationships and take care of our unfinished business. It's a time to explore inner horizons and to find forms of nourishment that may be quieter but are every bit as satisfying because they contribute to a sense of acceptance, wholeness, and peace of mind and heart. The intensity and drama of the earlier phases of life become less compelling precisely because the ego's need for recognition and control has been gentled into a wiser, more spacious and accepting way of relating to others and the world.

For many, this shift toward different life rhythms and a deeper interiority is not their way at all. For these people, the world of action will be their way until the end, their sails taut with wind, their lives governed by the will to action. Perhaps they'll be blessed by going down fast, dying with the wind in their sails and scarcely a thought to what I'm calling the shift.

Then there are others who may want to shift down but find it inconceivably difficult. They are the workaholics, locked in patterns of over-activity that drive them relentlessly. An empty calendar creates mild panic. "Who am I if not on the go all the time?" The reality of an identity crisis is too painful to endure, and so life in overdrive continues, perhaps until some physical crisis forces the inevitable.

I have written *Aging with Wisdom* particularly for those who feel inclined to slow down and look more deeply during the last phase of life and need some encouragement, a companion's voice on the journey, and tools for looking within. Truth be told, the modern Western world is a challenging environment for deep inner work.

In my opinion, something is seriously amiss in our culture. Materialism, consumerism, and the quest for youth combined with the fear of aging and denial of death make for a culture that is strangely arrested in an adolescent dream. When the later chapters of life are feared, elders demeaned, and the rejection of death come together, is it any wonder that there is such widespread depression among elders? We have been subtly—sometimes not so subtly—excised from the national psyche. A whole vital piece of the picture is missing. Elders who have been seasoned by life and earned their place as wayshowers and wisdom-givers are not granted the recognition and respect that is their due.

How different it is in most of Asia and among indigenous peoples where elders and ancestors are honored. Think of the ancestral altars in Asian homes, the Day of the Dead in Latin countries, Respect for the Aged day in Japan, or the role of elders in Native American culture where they are called the "wisdom keepers," a critical part of any council circle, always consulted when there are important decisions to be made. Women carried many leadership roles, nominated the confederacy chiefs, and counseled tribal governments. In fact, many tribal societies were matrilineal, tracing ancestry and inheriting status and wealth through the mothers. All of this ended when European settlers came in and destroyed almost every aspect of Native American culture.

In the Buddhist tradition, it is said that the moment of death is the most important. This may be a radical idea to us, but consider its implications. It is well known that those who live in fear, who have not healed the broken places in their lives, who haven't tended their unfinished business are often those for whom dying can be most difficult.

Buried in these stark facts is an invitation to do the inner work that calls to many of us more strongly in the later years. It is part of the tectonic inner shift—the call of the soul—to pay attention and heal the raw places in our lives. It's another kind of journey—surely as much a hero or heroine's journey as the outer forms it took in our younger years. This journey might not be as visible as the earlier one, but it is felt by all through an elder's presence and the quality of attention they bring to others. It is known through the fruits of their life experience now expressed as wisdom. It is recognized by new levels of acceptance, non-judgment, and compassion toward people and situations that stand in contrast to the sharp-edged, reactive, judgmental stances of earlier years. It is known by a sense that this elder is living more in the heart than in the head.

All of these attributes are healing. Sometimes a wise elder doesn't even need to speak, for the presence they embody carries its own quiet force. To those around, it may feel more like being in a safe, deep harbor, protected from the stormy waves of the sea of life. We need our elders. We need their acceptance, their wisdom, their compassion, and their love.

A New Vision

ONE WINTER DAY, walking along a slushy sidewalk in Montpelier, Vermont, I noticed an older woman walking ahead of me. She was taking measured steps, her gait slowed, her attention riveted on the simple act of walking. For her, walking was no longer a simple act; it took steady awareness of each step, scanning the sidewalk ahead for hidden ice, remembering to keep her weight over her feet; taking shorter steps, no longer the assured strides that once characterized her walking.

Others walked briskly past her, their gait sure, their stride long, as their purposeful walk propelled them toward their destination. She could hardly think about destination; for her, the immediacy of the moment was everything. She knew, at least subliminally, that a misstep could carry dire consequences. Concern over falling had become the new reality of her life.

What about those who passed her by? Had they noticed? Did they feel a flash of pity for her cautious steps, a twinge of anxiety over not wanting to become old and slow themselves? Did they dismiss her as another elder whose life was winding down toward greater infirmity? Or did they see with the eyes of compassion, a momentary flash of wishing her well, perhaps blessing her as they passed her by?

This image invites reflection. I am determined to look into the challenges of growing old in a culture that tends to dismiss its elderly as "over the hill," a burden to be borne. More than any other Western culture, the dominance of America's medical paradigm interprets the elder years as a medical problem. We need to recognize the reality of this view and ask ourselves how it compares with more traditional views of later life, where growing older has a gentler, kinder, respectful dimension.

The wise ones know better. Carl Jung referred to old age as the most valuable phase of life. I discovered this wonderful statement in one of the "Credos" written by Alice Howell, one of my wayshowers who appears later in the book, when she was in her late eighties. "There is no better reminder for our youth-centered world than Jung's casual remark that the most valuable period in life is Old Age. It is here, he implies, that the combination of values acquired in the first and second parts of our lives culminate and ideally, as from the fruit tree, the apples of our personal insights and wisdom fall as gifts to the collective unconscious. Taking the tree of life literally, every tree depends on root (first stage), growth (second), and giving forth (third), and looking back on the millennia of humankind, one can see nature's wisdom in recycling—also known as resurrection (or reincarnation)."[1]

But alas, the realities of aging in Western culture are very different from Jung's view. To give one of many possible examples, I have heard some of my friends, now elders, observe that they sometimes feel as though they've become invisible. Granted, in any gathering, people tend to be drawn to where the energy is strongest, and that is often with the young. But what happens to the place of the elder? Greg Mortenson, author of *Three Cups of Tea*, with his extraordinary work of building schools in Central Asia, asked a group of students in Pakistan how many had asked their grandparents to tell them stories about their lives. About ninety-five percent of them raised their hands. When he posed the same question to students in the U.S., only about five percent of the students' hands went up. What a striking contrast, he observed, between traditional societies and our country.

What internalized messages do elders live with because our culture is age phobic? What is it like to watch younger people dismiss them or make assumptions based more on fear than on reality? The prevalence of judgmental, negative attitudes toward the elderly must erode self-esteem and a sense of valued place in today's world.

How then do we accept the natural process of diminishment—our own diminishment? Starting with the issue of energy, if we are in our sixties or seventies, we have probably observed a gentle yet persistent process of slowing down beginning to govern our lives. Personally, I notice that my hands are slower to find correct change while those behind me in line for the checkout counter become impatient, that it takes longer to move through the tasks of starting the day—washing, getting dressed, tidying the room. I'm vigilant on stairs that I once bounced down vigorously and with assurance, because bifocals distort the relationship between steps, and I notice the shortness of breath as I climb the three flights of stairs to my study.

Just about everyone has moments of incredulity at the physical signs of their own aging. Recently I had such a moment while bending over when I saw with new eyes that my entire arm had become a symphony of wrinkles, and I stayed bent over, intrigued, amazed, studying the intricate patterns. Without so much as a thought, I heard myself speaking aloud, "Hello beautiful wrinkled arm," repeating the phrase three times, amazed at what this arm had become. Moments like these can be a source of merriment laced with melancholy, realizing that we're in an inexorable process yet struck with disbelief every time. We are now in "the wrinkled half of life," as Thomas Hardy described it. How whimsical, and true.

Diminishment, the gentle process of preparing us for another phase of life, is in the natural order of things. It is every bit as precious and valuable as the preceding chapters. Dear reader, do you protest at that statement? Understandably perhaps, but I believe we're being asked to look more deeply into the nature of the life cycle to discover the lessons that are embedded in the succession of losses, challenges, and sorrows. This is living consciously.

We are being invited to shift the lens through which we look upon the world. Is it possible to find a larger perspective, one that allows meaning in what otherwise seems ruthless or meaningless? In one way, we are surely "dwindling"—an affectionate term for the aging process. In another way, we are being invited to explore new ways of being. For example:

- Can we see the need to slow down as a gift, an example for those whose lives are squeezed by hurry?
- Can we see that acceptance of *being* in the present moment is as precious as *doing* in a society that measures according to how useful or productive a person is?
- Can we appreciate a sense of time that allows us to stop and enjoy a small delight like the iridescence on the anemone petal in the flower arrangement someone gave us?
- Can we accept the gift of time—time to be—to watch the play of wind in the trees outside the window instead of simply rushing on to the next task?
- Is it possible that we're being invited to live in a new dimension, one that is teaching us to let go of the way we've always done things? Ultimately, we are moving toward the final letting go whether we are conscious of it or not. Death may be years off, but every time we let go of an old pattern, we open to a more spacious, allowing, and loving way of being.

Why is that loving? you might wonder. Any act of letting go involves loving, because as we do so, we live more in alignment with our essential Self. We become more accepting of the unknown, more open to the great mystery in which we live and into which we shall die.

I'll always be indebted to Teilhard de Chardin for his wisdom on this subject. A priest, philosopher, poet, and mystic, he described in *The Divine Milieu* that in our younger years one is invited to "divinize one's activities," whereas in the later phases of life the invitation is to "divinize one's passivities" or "hallow one's diminishments."

I originally heard his statement referred to simply as "the grace of diminishment." Though only in my early forties at the time, I was so struck by the power of his words, I copied them out, went home, and started a file that I titled "Wisdom and Aging." For me, this phrase is a "wisdom treasure." Some might balk at the idea of diminishment. Who wants it? But it is an inevitable part of life, so, as with any challenge that comes our way, how do we find ways to make meaning out of it?

At various times during the six years that I accompanied my husband through his journey with Alzheimer's disease, I pondered these words. One might wonder how there can be any grace in mental loss, but we found it. Usually in the smallest things: the blessing of family and friends who offered support; the laughter over confused words; the comfort of hand holding hand; the appreciation of what remained in spite of heartbreaking losses; above all, an amplified sense of life's preciousness as he was moving toward death.

We all know that Alzheimer's is a ruthless disease, devastating for the patient and their family, tedious, exhausting, heart-rending, financially draining, filled with loss and grief. Those are the realities. But there is also the possibility of finding grace in diminishment, an invitation to shift our lens to affirm what is positive.

When Hob was in the middle stages of Alzheimer's, I remember a sweet moment when, with a satisfied smile, he said simply, "It's really nice to be old."

How often do you hear someone say those words? I loved hearing him say that. It felt like a gift, a surprising affirmation of where he was even though he was dealing with the gradual loss of his mind.

Another inspiring example of shifting the lens comes from the writer John Yungblut, Quaker by tradition, who made the hallowing of his diminishments the spiritual practice by which he negotiated his physical decline with Parkinson's. He wrote honestly about the shock and resistance he felt upon learning his diagnosis. Denial, disbelief, despair, depression, fear—these too are part of our humanness. We ignore them at our peril, because in some way we need to go through the fire of afflictive emotions to burn through to some new, unimagined way of relating to what is happening. None of us is ever ready for a life-threatening diagnosis, and so we must bring great compassion to whatever hurricane of emotions is let loose by the inevitability of decline and death. We must honor the storm so we can clear the turbulence for a clearer vision that hopefully will follow.

After finding a place of acceptance of the Parkinson's, Yungblut practiced imagining his diminishment as a companion that would accompany him all the way to the final diminishment of death. In a stunning example of reframing a situation, he began to see that the *rigor mortis* that his body would undergo at death could be preceded by the practice of seeing the gradual stiffening of Parkinson's as "a kind of *rigor amoris*—a stiffening by love," as he put it, that would eventually lead him to dying into God, for that was his belief about death.

What an inspiring example of how to hallow one's diminishments. The aging process asks us—demands, in fact—that we find a larger perspective, something beyond just focusing on physical loss, by which to negotiate illness. This is what de Chardin meant by hallowing one's passivities and diminishments. This means that the process of aging is another chapter in the sacred journey of life. How can one say that the process of aging is sacred? What a counterintuitive idea. Even more, a countercultural idea. How can we accept that proposition when aging also includes heartbreaking losses, pain, and sorrow? As we struggle through the challenges of physical loss—that first line of care that must be addressed—we're also being invited to shift dimensions. We need to pay more attention to larger perspectives. How do we find meaning in suffering? What practices—like prayer and meditation—can sustain us? Where do we find bits of inspiration to uplift us?

On the subtle levels, we are being presented with opportunities for new responses: the call for acceptance of things as they are; the invitation to accept the help of others, a daunting challenge for fiercely independent types; the possibility that we open to the realm of spirit, to see loss and decline with new eyes, not through the impatient eyes of judgment, but with a heart that can hold everything that's happening, including death; and finally, the sense that we're part of something far more spacious than the limitations of the physical body.

In our last years when we're in decline, most of us will be confronted with the most challenging health issues of our lives. If you think about those people who have inspired you by how they handled their final illness and death, not only are they your role models or wayshowers; they are the heroines and heroes of their own lives. Our culture may still have a way to go before accepting this view, but it's there as possibility, as encouragement, as inspiration.

This leads us, dear reader, to reflect on how other cultures look at the life cycle and aging, not to emulate unfamiliar forms but to open to their wisdom. Surely cultivating openness to the new and unknown is one of the secrets to a dynamic old age.

The next few sections include examples of what we can learn from other cultures, archetypal approaches to aging, and an inspiring example of a program designed to meet the needs of its elders.

Honoring the Life Cycle

WHEN I FIRST learned about the four stages of life as set forth in Indian Vedic philosophy, I was impressed by a culture that acknowledged these phases and provided guidelines for living wisely. According to these teachings, the four stages are called *ashramas*, a word that means "shelter," suggesting that we take *shelter* in each of the phases throughout our life.

The movement from one *ashrama* to another presupposes a spiritual perspective on the purpose of life, namely that we live in accordance with dharmic laws and follow practices that lead us from primarily identifying with our limited self, or ego, to gradually identifying with our true Self, the divinity within. This process eventually leads to liberation or enlightenment, which in that culture is perceived as the ultimate purpose of life. Though a long way from the modern person's view, it is still embedded in traditional Hindu philosophy and still has an influence in that culture.

The first stage is called *Brahmacharya* and refers to the "student" phase of life, when education dominates one's first twenty or so years. The next twenty-five years or so are called *Grihasta*, meaning the "householder" stage where we may marry and raise a family, but it also includes our work in the world and is sometimes referred to as the "marketplace" stage.

The third stage, known at *Vanaprastha*, is the one most relevant for those of us who are aging. After the student and householder stages, this stage is called the "forest monk" stage, when your children are adults and your career has reached fruition. It is time to pay more attention to reflection, contemplation, and the inner life. Generally, this is the decade between fifty and sixty when our children have left home, when we may have our first grey hairs (or maybe many, and much earlier!), when we may feel the impulse to simplify our life and shed some of our material possessions. Furthermore, in this stage of life, we may be serving in the role of mentors.

The fourth and final stage is called *Sannyasa*, a word that means "renunciation." This is for the few who would ordain and devote themselves fully to the spiritual life as monastics do. Although this progression may feel very foreign to us, there is wisdom encoded in this Vedic view of the life cycle. If affirms the natural shift from the fast-forward living of the middle years to the gentler rhythms of growing older, and it validates those of us who feel an inclination toward honoring the inner life more than has been possible while we've been focused on our work and family obligations.

In relating to this Vedic paradigm, I sometimes delight in telling certain friends that I'm trying to honor the forest monk stage of life. There is a chuckle of recognition from some people as I tell about these four stages of life, an appreciation for a system that validates what is important to them as well. Clearly this is not the way for many people, especially those who will work at full tilt until something stops them in their tracks. But for those of us who are drawn to a more contemplative life, there is a chuckle of recognition from those I tell, as well as appreciation for a system that validates what is important to them too. It isn't possible for many to scale back their work schedules or leave the workplace as the third stage invites, but cultivating the practice of renunciation is possible at any time, in any circumstance, as long as one understands its deeper meaning.

In its deepest sense, renunciation refers to the longing for freedom. One's spiritual practice becomes the organizing principle of one's life. That priority may not be on our radar screen at all, or some might think it means leaving the secular life and being cloistered away in some monastery. But no, it's about cultivating an attitude of letting go or surrender toward how we are living at all levels—material, emotional, mental, and spiritual. For many, this is the main calling of our later years.

On the material level, it means looking at our lifetime of accumulated things to see what we can give away, how we can downsize and simplify. Having watched my mother nearly broken by clearing out a spacious Victorian house lived in for three generations, I vowed never to leave a nightmare of material excess for my children to deal with at my death.

The deeper meaning of renunciation invites us to live with greater awareness of our subtler forms of attachment—to afflictive emotions like anger, pride, or impatience; compulsive behaviors around food, shopping, or media; and, trickiest of all, negative mind states like worrying, self-doubt, or judgment. At still another level, we can soften and let go around self-cherishing tendencies and recognize the happiness that comes when preoccupation with self gives way to deeper caring for others.

The essential question is how we honor the life cycle and live more attuned to the rhythms appropriate to our years. When we are "attuned," we know when we're living in balance with the natural order of things and aligned with our life's purpose. This is a process of deep listening, respecting our changing needs, and honoring what is truly most important to us. To support this process, a beloved friend of mine, a Congregational minister named Charles Busch, created a unique program to provide support and inspiration for the elders in his congregation. The program turned out to be so intriguing, many younger members participated as well. He called it "ElderSpirit."

ELDERSPIRIT

B Y HIS MIDDLE years, my friend Charles had already had several careers—writer, fundraiser, Public Relations Manager for Volkswagen in five Southwestern states, and partner in an engineering firm. Even though he had explored these various options for work, he still felt a deep uneasiness about what he was doing with his life. As the proverbial image goes, he had arrived on the ladder of success only to discover that it was leaning against the wrong wall. Something else was now calling.

He decided to take some time off to reflect on his life and consider his next steps. He went on a four-months solitary retreat at Nova Nada, the former Benedictine monastery in Nova Scotia, to pray, meditate, and write. Out of the silence and solitude arose his new sense of direction. He refers to this as the "Jesus intrusion," for with a radical change of direction, he decided to enroll in divinity school. After completing his degree, he became a minister in the United Church of Christ, going first into a rural parish ministry in Tombstone, Arizona and eventually ended up guiding a large, engaged congregation in Lincoln City, Oregon.

When he arrived at the church in Lincoln City, he discovered that the congregation was almost entirely composed of "gray heads," as he described them. Parishioners expressed their regrets about this, and his first assignment from the church leaders was to attract more young families and children, "a reasonable request and crucial to our future," he told me. He continued to explain what unfolded.

"Looking out at all those gray heads during worship one Sunday, I had a tiny epiphany: They are so beautiful! I remembered studying Hinduism at Divinity School and how people in that tradition look forward to the third stage of life—the forest dwelling years—when they can turn from family responsibilities and serving community to concentrate on their spiritual life.

"Suddenly the emphasis of my ministry became one of learning together what it means to be an elder. Soon I saw what we came to call 'ElderSpirit' education as crucial to the baby-boomer population and our nation's soul."

My husband Hob and I met Charles and became close friends during his divinity school years. Some years later, when the time came for his first sabbatical, he returned to the East Coast on a fellowship to Harvard Divinity School, his alma mater. That's when he came up with an intriguing proposal for a program that he would eventually name ElderSpirit. It would address some of the issues that arise in midlife and become compelling with age, with an emphasis on spiritual life.

The format was to meet for three or four weekends a year to explore an inspiring series of topics such as "Re-imaging Age" to reframe our culture's bias against growing older and re-focus on the positive aspects of this rich stage of life. Another weekend was devoted to "Finding Hope After Loss" to explore ways of relearning joy following significant losses, including loved ones, dreams, goals, vitality, and options. There was a weekend entitled "Death, the Final Stage of Growth," with the purpose of exploring how we might approach our own death free of fear, secure in faith, and awake to the blessings of each moment. "Telling our Stories: Spirituality and Life Review" was about finding the deeper meaning in the stories that have formed our lives so we can begin to treasure our life experiences and embrace the opportunities of aging.

These were just a few of the many intriguing topics that became the offerings of the ElderSpirit program. As Charles put it, "The approach of inviting prophets from out-of-town to come to Lincoln City to speak to elders and interested youngers worked," as people of diverse ages, from their forties to nineties, came together for these spirited weekends of talks, discussion groups, and deep sharing.

Finally, as one of the countless gifts of ElderSpirit, Charles had expressed his vision for the program in a compelling statement. With these words, he describes the essence of what it means to be an elder. How marvelous it would be if this statement were crafted into a beautiful, framed picture that hung in the front hall of every elder community, assisted living complex, and nursing home.

ElderSpirit

We are the mentors, the wisdom keepers.
We are the ones who bestow the
blessings of spiritual legacy.
We are the survivors with a story to tell
that can save others.
We are the ones who serve notice
it is possible to transcend "doing"
in favor of "being."
We are the models of what it means to
arrive wounded and triumphant at the end.
We are the mapmakers for the final
uncharted part of the journey.
We are the elders.

ARCHETYPES OF AGING

S OONER OR LATER, almost everyone of a certain age repeats the same refrain: "How did I get here?!" We find that we are in the middle of a paradox: our physical age is only an undisputed numerical measurement, whereas our sense of Self—our spirit or true nature—feels ageless, as though we're still somewhere in our twenties or thirties.

One of the persistent challenges of this discrepancy between our age and our self-image is that it's hard to accept this new reality. We simply can't believe we're in the realm of older age. For example, we imagine that we can still play tennis as we did in our twenties, and then we end up throwing our back out. We push ourselves to the same rigorous schedules as in our forties and find ourselves exhausted day after day. Determined to show how independent we are, we refuse a friend's arm going down stairs and end up nearly falling.

How natural to experience ambivalent feelings about aging. I carry contradictory images in my psyche between those who thrive into their later years and those who are broken by it. I have the vibrant, warrior-like energy of my paternal grandmother who, in her eighties, undertook a monumental writing project to refute the inaccurate historical account about her father, Adelbert Ames, the reconstruction Governor of Mississippi, as told in John F. Kennedy's *Profiles in Courage*. After receiving a letter from my grandmother in which she pointed out the errors, Kennedy refused to revise his book with the explanation that there would be no further editions. Undaunted, she decided to prove him wrong. She started a five-year research and writing project.

Her book, lavishly illustrated, meticulously footnoted, and scholarly turned out to be 578 pages long.

At one point, when her son—my father—came to visit, he asked her how the project was coming along and how many pages she'd written.

"It's over 500 pages, and I'm still not finished," she replied.

"Mother, don't you think that's getting long enough?"

She drew herself up to her full, though somewhat diminished height, and replied forcefully, "If Tolstoy could do it, so can I!"

Her impressive tome created a ripple among American historians to the extent that my graduate school professor urged me to write my thesis on the same subject to verify the legitimacy of her claims. I didn't. But her scholarly research was affirmed. The book still stands as a testament to her determination and energy, stunning at that stage of her life. It is now shelved in university libraries along with the books of leading scholars in American history.

By contrast, I have a friend for whom old age seems more like a sentence to be endured. Her life has closed in, its horizons narrowed with one day almost identical to another, her spiritedness dimmed. Alas, this is the reality for many, especially if they're struggling with chronic illness, financial woes, loneliness, and the inevitable losses.

There is a compelling difference between the physical decline that naturally comes with years and the broken spiritedness that colonizes the lives of many. There are ample reasons for discouragement and depression—over limitations, curtailed capacities, physical pain, personal losses, over life lost. Yet think of those you know who, in spite of the foregoing, are still engaged with life, vibrant, with lively minds, spirited by nature.

Our age-denying culture sets the odds against the elderly. Too often they are ignored, dismissed, segregated, or rendered invisible by the ageism that pervades our national psyche.

Unlike many cultures, we in modern America lack images and archetypes that can guide us in our elder years. Without images to constellate the mixed feelings we naturally have about aging, feelings go underground, into the unconscious where they fester as aversion, revulsion, denial, fear, and so on. Those feelings then leak out or erupt in negative humor, subtle put-downs, and caricatures of the aging. This kind of unconscious denigration would never happen in cultures that respect the elderly.

I recently heard an inspiring account of living in one of those cultures that deeply respects its elders. David is a new friend, a retired pilot. When his wife Nerina was diagnosed with Alzheimer's, they decided to move to Phnom Penh, Cambodia, to be close to their only son. He described the last five years of Nerina's life as being the happiest years of their life together. How could anyone make such a startling, unlikely statement? Having lived through the enormous challenges of my husband declining into Alzheimer's, I asked him to elaborate on his experience.

David explained that it had everything to do with Cambodian culture, with its deeply held values of love and respect for elders. Wherever they went, he said, people welcomed Nerina as though she were their beloved mother. They would enter a neighborhood restaurant and the headwaiter would come up to Nerina and give her a hug. Her meal would arrive and someone would be there kneeling beside her chair helping to feed her before David could even lift a fork to help her. It didn't matter that Nerina spoke little or sometimes not at all. She smiled. She felt welcomed, accepted, and loved. Words weren't necessary; the loving attention was all that mattered, and that's what the Cambodians were eager to give, especially to an older woman who was clearly impaired.

As to his own experiences in Cambodia, David described a moment when he himself felt unsteady going down stairs in a public place. He started to reach for the bannister, and instantly the person nearest to him reached out and gave him support. With a chuckle, he called it "the white hair syndrome." Because of his white hair, Cambodians seemed to have a second sense for when help might be needed. With their highly attuned antennae toward the elderly, invariably upon seeing David, they would greet him with some welcoming words. When he went out to buy bread in the early morning, the tip tip drivers, who drove the three-wheeled, open-air taxis, would call out to him, "Good morning Papa! Good morning!" What a heartwarming salutation with which to start the day!

Wherever they went, whatever the circumstances, David said they felt welcomed, supported, and loved. To be so fully embraced by the people of another culture provided a sense of being included and deeply appreciated, *because* they were elders in a culture that reveres its old people. And the depth of those positive qualities seemed to eclipse the difficulties of dementia.

As I listened to David describe their lives in Cambodia, I felt wistful about our culture. Although it is encouraging to see an expanding literature about aging and photographic collections with essays that celebrate creative older people, we still have a long way to go to reverse the negative projections directed at elders in this country.

I have found it intriguing to explore images that portray the realities of aging. Images carry their own power to touch the deeper levels of the psyche—beyond the rational mind—and broaden the perspective and meaning that we bring to life experience. In some cultures, these images come in the form of archetypes, specifically as goddesses. Archetypes are evocative insofar as they are symbolic representations of psychological processes. They account for the power of myths and fairy tales and explain why these stories, timeless and compelling, are embedded in our memory. We dismiss the wisdom encoded in these archetypes at our peril, for they work at far deeper levels of the psyche than ordinary images or concepts.

Why goddesses? Women are traditionally seen as midwives of both birth and death—the great mysteries—and it's the feminine principle (in both men and women) that is regarded as the receptive, intuitive, and mysterious dimension of human experience. Archetypes reveal the hidden processes of inner life and make them conscious, inviting reflection and acceptance.

One of the most familiar archetypal images of old age is the Crone of the Triple Goddess. Fortunately, the women's movement has begun to reclaim this archetype, but for many it still evokes pejorative reactions, undoubtedly a left-over from the millennium of patriarchy where the power of the feminine was attacked from every direction. The root of the word "crone," however, comes from the word "crown," suggesting a very different way to regard the late years as the "crowning" of a life.

The crone is not to be denigrated but embraced, for she is often seen as a grandmother figure, wisdom keeper, wayshower, healer, or seer. Crone goddess figures are also associated with freedom and even wildness, because a new courage or inner strength may dawn in old age, born from a lifetime of hard-won experience.

There is a kaleidoscope of images from goddess cultures, for example, the truth of Dhumavati, which I describe in some detail later in the book. To give some examples, we hear of a warrior crone goddess who symbolizes wisdom, inspiration, and the cycle of life and death (Irish); another goddess of life, death, and immortality (Native American); a goddess of longevity, protection, and psychic abilities (Japanese); a guardian of women's mysteries (Hebrew); another who understands the nature of death (Celtic); and one last, chosen from a much longer list, who is associated with death, magic, and reincarnation (Egyptian).

What's striking about the number of crone goddesses is how many cultures around the world have sought ways to represent this crowning stage of the life cycle. They show the wisdom of embracing the cycles that must wholeheartedly include death. That's why Dhumavati, the goddess of old age from India, is such a compelling figure. She is repellant, ruthless, and dark, robbing body and mind of robustness—a reminder of decline, disintegration, and death. I was surprised and strangely relieved to learn about an archetype that portrays the truth so powerfully.

I'm struck by the richness of these archetypes. Archetypes may assume forms that arise from their particular cultures, but their energy and meaning are universal. These figures include a spectrum of empowering qualities such as freedom, wildness, wisdom, inspiration, and psychic abilities, all wonderful to celebrate in our later years. As well, archetypal images are associated with the mysteries of birth, death, rebirth, and immortality. Their power is available to anyone open to their symbolism, and they offer an invitation for us to cultivate healthy perspectives toward old age.

Turning to a somewhat different example, Dogen, a thirteenth century Zen master in Japan, offers another inspiring description from the elder years, the grandmother's heart.

THE MIND OF
GREAT COMPASSION

"You can understand all of Buddhism, but you cannot go
beyond your abilities and your intelligence unless you have
robai-shin, grandmother mind, the mind of great compassion."
–EIHEI DOGEN (1200-1253, founder of
the Soto School of Zen Buddhism)

WHEN I FIRST heard Dogen's simple yet powerful words,
I was stirred to the core. *Robai-shin* describes the expansive state of mind that is the fruit of a lifetime of experience.
In East Asian languages, mind and heart are designated by the
same word, *shin*. The grandmother's heart has been broken open
and healed countless times through the hard knocks of her life.
In through the cracks of disappointment and pain come compassion and loving-kindness. Compassion, an all-embracing love
that excludes nothing, arises naturally. Whether the travails of a
grandchild or the ravages of our planet, it is all gathered into the
arms of grandmotherly compassion.

Along with compassion comes wisdom. The two are the
ultimate treasure of the Buddhist tradition, and with them
comes the gift of presence. Our presence as grandmothers
is no longer about work or career, although we may still be
as engaged in work as ever, but about the quality of presence—the ability to be *with* life in all its complexity, joys, and
sorrows, with things as they are, with our grandchildren, our
children, and our community and planet with a heart as wide
as the world.

Perhaps there is an echo of *robai-shin* in some Native American traditions where it was the old women who chose the next chief of the tribe—not the younger warriors, not the power grabbers, not the seconds-in-command, but the old women. Imagine living in a culture that honors its elder women in this manner.

Dogen's statement is radical, groundbreaking. He honors the reality of grandmother mind with full respect. I find it hard to imagine a statement like his being made in our times. Our culture is fraught with ageism, often hidden but inferred—by tone of voice, by the assumed superiority of the young, by demeaning statements about elders and what it means to be old in a youth-obsessed world. Furthermore, unlike some other cultures, we lack archetypes for honoring the elderly, sacred feminine.

Dogen describes the grandmother's heart as having "great compassion." Why? Because age—that ultimate gift—gives us perspectives on life that are inconceivable to the young. It offers us—all grandmothers, all elders—the possibility of cultivating the heart of boundless compassion.

May *robai-shin*, grandmother mind, the mind of great compassion, touch the hearts of all beings.

A Grandmother's Gift

SHE'S SITTING ON *a stool in front of her dressing table in the alcove off the master bedroom. Light floods in through the windows at her back. I see the trees outside the windows reflected in the three-sided mirror on the dressing table as well as three different views of her face. She is brushing out her long, white hair with slow, caring strokes. Her hair is all wavy from the braids she weaves every morning. Enthralled, I watch as she winds the braids into a crown on top of her head, and secures them in place with long, silver hairpins.*

"There, all done," she says and turns toward me, smiles tenderly, and reaches out to take my hand. I look down at her hand. It is fair-skinned, almost translucent, with its raised rivers of bluish veins. They intrigue me. Sometimes I ask her to hold still while I press down on one of the big ones, seeing if I can make that river of blood dam up or stop. I can't.

"Always brush your hair a lot and then it will shine," she explains. "And here, let me do yours," and she reaches for the brush and starts on my long, blond hair, also braided every morning but with the braids left down to bounce freely on my back.

Something about the brushing makes me feel dreamy, safe, cared for. As my grandmother, Beep, brushes, deeply engaged in this ancient women's ritual of hairdressing, she reminisces about her childhood home in Denmark, about the enclosed farmyard with its ducks and chickens, the thatched roof, the blue larkspur that stood against the whitewashed walls. I'm transported to another land, intriguing and mysterious.

My maternal grandmother was the first person that I remember as old. There were the obvious things like her white hair, her blue-veined hands, the wrinkles around her eyes and mouth, the slowed step. She was beautiful, but as a sensitive child, I sensed something more. Underneath her aging beauty, her wonderful storytelling, and her abiding love for me, I felt a sadness about her. I couldn't have put the pieces together back then, but maybe life had inflicted its secret wounds, deep and hidden. Perhaps it was some distant hurt, disappointment, or lack of fulfillment. Maybe it was the marriage.

Life inflicts its wounds, hidden or not, on all of us, to a greater or lesser degree. There's no escaping that reality. Yet there's always the possibility of redemption. Life invites us to heal those wounds. How we do that is our unique path to follow. As we move into our later years, these issues become more urgent. These reflections arose many years after my grandmother's death, but our precious connection endures. In fact, these ruminations arose *because* of who she was. Something about the sensitivity that we shared is timeless, and about how protected I felt in her presence. Most memorable was how I felt *seen* by her.

I am in my grandparent's garden. It must be June, because the irises—the ebullient, purple variety—are in full, radiant bloom at the back of the garden. Behind the irises stands a hemlock hedge, dark green, almost black, stirring slightly in the warm afternoon wind. The birdbath by the iris bed is a-flurry with activity, mainly sparrows jockeying for position with their splashing, flying drops, feather rufflings.

The bird activity intrigues me. I'm seven years old, a rather quiet, inward child who wonders about many things that grown-ups don't seem to talk about. I've been sitting in the grass, watching the birds, until I hear my grandmother Beep's voice calling me. She settles into the white wicker chair nearby and extends her arm to draw me close.

Her eyes, faintly milky with age, are a brilliant blue. Her white hair is, as always, braided and pinned into a crown around her head. She holds me close as we observe the birds together. Gently she releases me to kneel in the grass beside her chair.

I don't remember what words may have passed between us, but I will never forget how she looked at me—her long, lingering gaze, radiating totally unconditional love.

Why should I remember that moment so vividly? Was it because people seldom look at one another in that open, wholehearted way, without judgments, expectations, or conditions to their love? Do elders appreciate life's preciousness because death shadows them more closely? Is it because they have the time to look and allow their hearts to love boundlessly?

Two such simple moments from over seventy years ago. When I think about my grandmother, her presence and unconditional love continue to be treasured memories, for relationships don't end when someone dies; they assume a different form. Some aspects of the relationship become more vivid while others fade. In some way, the presence of that person still occupies a place in the psyche. As I ponder this subject, it leads inevitably to the mystery of time and how it relates to aging.

THE MYSTERY OF TIME

M Y HUSBAND, NOW drifting into the middle stages of living with Alzheimer's, was sitting on the back stairs playing with the shoelaces of his grungy old sneakers. We were getting ready to leave for his appointment, but he was floating, or so it felt to me, in some timeless cocoon. He had already forgotten, totally unaware that we needed to leave.

I was standing by the door. I felt impatience rising. I was responsible for everything now, including getting him to appointments on time. I reminded him that we needed to go, that we were going to be late. The pressure of time. Again.

Sensing my frustration, he looked up slowly from the interminable process of tying his shoelaces. *More like a three-year old than a seventy-three-year old*, I thought to myself. With a slightly mischievous expression, he declared, "This stage of life is all about 'slowth.' It's about getting *down* to speed."

He repeated the words "*down* to speed," emphasizing the word "down" as if he were training our dog.

I got the message. In fact, I never forgot it. In his own way, he—the lifelong teacher—was still teaching.

That was one of many times when I felt the startling discrepancy between his slowing down and my usual determined pace. With his observation about "slowth," with its faint echo with the word "sloth" (indeed sloths go *very* slowly), I realized how much we were now living in different time zones. It became a practice for me to learn how to adjust my rhythms to his, a practice that anyone who works with elders knows well.

Aging and time become inseparable issues. I no longer feel that I have "all the time in the world," that popular expression seldom heard in modern day, time-pressed lives. As I move into my late seventies, time seems to fly by ever more rapidly. Yet, from a moment-to-moment perspective, time feels as if it's going slower. What a paradox. Because many years have accrued behind me, it creates the illusion that time is passing faster. Nothing has changed except my perception of time.

What influences our experience of time? The ancient Greeks used two words to explain different aspects of time: the word *chronos*—chronological or linear time, the one that governs our lives and sometimes drives us crazy—and *kairos*—vertical time, those timeless moments when we experience the eternal. When we're living fully in the present, eternity is embedded in every passing moment.

Meister Eckhart, the Christian mystic, said much the same thing when he wrote about that "place" in the soul that is eternal. And the well-known Biblical saying, "Be still and know" also refers to *kairos*, the sense of timelessness. In that stillness, we access deeper levels of knowing, insight, and wisdom.

As I ponder the mystery of time, linear time—especially when we feel pressed about it—is linked to the sense of a solid self, that ego which is very busy managing our lives. The ego wants things in its own way, in its own time. Just think how many instances of impatience are driven by this driving sense of trying to control time.

To bring in another perspective, in the Buddhist tradition it is said that we live between the two realms of desire and aversion, what we want and what we don't want. Both involve fantasies about the future, always wishing that something in our lives would be different. Look at all the expressions we have about time and urgency: "the race against time," "beat the clock," "never enough time," "time pressure," "time management," "killing time," "deadlines, "don't waste time"—the examples multiply endlessly.

When we're deeply absorbed in an activity we love or in meditation, we slip into the vertical dimension of time—*kairos*—where we feel most truly at home with ourselves, with the activity, and with the world around us. We're beyond ego. We're free. We can slip into *kairos* time whenever we choose. Even in a simple moment of coming home to ourselves, there is an experience of vivid presence, wholeness, and well-being. Significantly, in this meditative moment, there is freedom from the usual busyness of the mind.

An arresting story illustrates how some cultures refuse to surrender their relationship to time; indigenous people tend to respect life's natural rhythms and honor the importance of inner time, or soul time. Bruce Chatwin, a white explorer in Africa, hired a team of black porters to carry provisions across the continent by a certain deadline. After several days of nonstop walking, the men insisted on stopping for a break. Chatwin tried to persuade them to continue. He cajoled them. He pressured them. Finally he offered them cash. And then still more cash, but the men refused to move. One of them finally explained to Chatwin, "They are waiting for their souls to catch up."[2]

As elders we may begin to have different perspectives on time. Concepts about time might take on a new urgency. Our time is running out. I wanted to understand how the years could speed by while each day seem wondrously slow. One explanation is that for an eleven-year-old child, one day is approximately 1/4,000th of his or her life, whereas to a fifty-five-year old, one day would be about 1/20,000th of his or her life. This five-fold discrepancy might help explain why perceptions about time vary so dramatically between the young and the old.

An experiment sheds further light on the subject; it compared subjects aged nineteen to twenty-four with another group aged sixty to eighty. When asked to estimate when three minutes had passed, the younger group's answers averaged between three minutes and three seconds whereas the elders estimated that three minutes and forty seconds had passed, an illuminating difference.[3]

Busy. That loaded, time-related word! How often people tell us how busy they are. Too busy to have lunch. Too busy to go for a walk. Too busy to talk now. Busyness seems to be a status symbol in our culture, a way of measuring one's importance by how busy you are. At the turn of the twentieth century, the philosopher William James, while writing about our potential for depth and integrity, added, "But that potential is lost when your days are spread so thin that busyness is your true occupation."[4]

Thomas Merton, the Trappist monk, prolific author, and mystic, referred to "our busyness as a pervasive form of contemporary violence." If you reflect on those times in your daily life when you're consumed by busyness, doesn't it feel as though you've compromised your inner balance, no longer aligned with the rhythms of the natural world?

An illuminating cross-cultural example comes from the Chinese language in which the character or pictogram for "busy" has two parts; one represents the word for "heart," the other the word for "killing." Heart killing. What a descriptive phrase, for that's how we often feel when rushing from one activity to another, lost in the pressures of relentless doing, driven by the feeling that there is never enough time. In the midst of our over-busyness, we may feel as though we've lost heart. As the Chinese say, if you're preoccupied with past or future, thus missing the present moment, you're "killing life."

Many Asian cultures embrace a cyclical view of time. Indian culture, in particular, has vast perspectives on time. The word *kalpa* refers to ages that are comprised of billions of years, and the human soul is seen as cycling through these kalpas or eons on its way to reaching final realization or liberation, to escape the wheel of time, regarded by these traditions as the purpose of human birth.

In the elder years, as our sense of time shifts, it's not only that we feel how precious time is, but we find ourselves looking back over our lives from a new perspective. This may include the process of harvesting our lives—wanting to savor memories, heal what is unfinished, and reflect on the choices and turning points that have created the arc of our life. If we've retired from the workplace and live our days free from external structures and time pressures, we may notice that time now seems more spacious, almost malleable. Past and future seem to be woven into the present in new ways. Something about the aging process softens our attitudes toward time so that we experience it as being more circular than linear.

For elders, our gentler rhythms make the speediness of the young feel intrusive, even overwhelming. Youth's fast forward pace, so natural to where they are in the life cycle, now feels dissonant with the slower pace of being older. If an elder is experiencing a decline in energy, illness, or dementia, the natural process of slowing down calls for matching the gentler rhythms of the elderly. It means speaking more slowly and attuning one's presence to theirs. We live in different time zones, so to speak.

Even though the young and the old experience different relationships to time, we still share many of the same universal issues. What gives life meaning? Who am I now that I've moved into a different life stage? What are my priorities? Whether forty, seventy, or ninety, these are still the core questions. How poignant that we can share so deeply even while feeling the chasm between our realities.

With one further reflection about time, we need only remember that our ultimate refuge is in the present moment. David Whyte, the American poet with deep Celtic roots, reminds us of the place where we experience freedom from the constraints of time, and invites us there in his poem titled *Enough*.

> Enough. These few words are enough.
> If not these words, this breath.
> If not this breath, this sitting here.
>
> This opening to the life
> we have refused
> again and again
> until now.
>
> Until now.[5]

This leads us to a timeless, almost dreamlike interlude that I experienced in a most unexpected place, in a form I could never have anticipated.

A Wordless Encounter

I've always loved traveling by train, anywhere, anytime. Once, not long ago, I was on a train from Taunton in southern England to the bustling city of Birmingham, three hours north through the incomparably beautiful, rural countryside.

I settled into my seat, rustled through my carry-on to find my reading, then ignored it. Instead I gazed dreamily out the window watching the landscape pass by. As always I was struck how the fields were graced by sheep, cows, and horses; the abundance of animal life enlivened the landscape in a most heartwarming way.

Animals were everywhere. Their presence declared that here in the English countryside, all was well with the world. Tall, thick hedgerows of hawthorn entangled with blackberry separated one well-grazed field from another. Here and there a great oak rose to declare its mighty presence. When the villages appeared, almost all of them were contained within discreet boundaries with very little of the sprawl that disfigures the larger towns.

The sound of the speeding train plus the passing landscape lulled me into a contented state. The train stopped at the first station where an older woman, well into her eighties, boarded and awkwardly settled into the seat across the aisle from me. She was trying to decide whether to put her luggage up on the rack or leave it on the seat beside her. She was traveling alone, and I sensed that she was challenged by the unfamiliar circumstances. I waited to see if she needed help.

Then a mysterious process began to unfold. I imagined the presence of someone in the seat next to me, a woman in her early sixties who was struggling to accept her own aging and harboring unconscious ageism. I imagined that as she watched the old woman across the aisle, she was feeling vaguely uncomfortable. The old woman was a reminder of her own aging, that she too would one day be old, maybe much like this very woman whom she was watching.

A series of phrases began to unfold in my mind as I silently spoke to my seatmate:

"Don't deplore your aging body;
    It is your natural inheritance.

Don't judge your folds of flesh;
    Rather thank your body for how it has supported you.

Don't take your eyes from the old woman who sits opposite you;
    Her world is your world;
    You only reside in an earlier time.

Don't deplore her slower movements, her repetitive gestures;
    She's confirming the reliability of an increasingly uncertain world.

Don't trumpet your superiority in relation to her;
    She is here to show you where you are going.
    Her presence alone can teach you acceptance of age.

Don't feel sorry for her because she's old;
    Her world is as precious to her as yours is to you.

Don't dismiss her because she just sits there apparently doing nothing;
    She's showing you how to be in this moment.

Don't let the pain of separation deceive you;
    You are not separate; it's only your mind that creates separation.

Don't throw her out of your heart because she is old;
    She is your mother, your sister.
    She is you."

I appreciated the wisdom rising unbidden, while the woman across the aisle remained unaware that I was in touch with her through my imaginings. The words had arisen from my passion to stand up for the elderly in a culture that renders them invisible, dismissing them with judgments. I was surprised by my own quiet passion and wordlessly thanked the woman across the aisle. She'd given me a gift about which she knew nothing. How mysteriously we are interconnected.

Half an hour passed, and the conductor announced the next station. I watched my elderly neighbor rise to leave the train, her movements slow and careful as she turned to walk down the aisle. Curious to know what was going to happen to her, through the window I watched a young couple with two eager children come to greet her. Each one took their turn for a hug. She had arrived safely into the embrace of family.

Meanwhile, I quietly mused at the unexpected inner dialogue that her presence had invited. I'm always grateful for the silent camaraderie of the elderly. With the sound of the whistle and a gentle lurch, the train started to move, and I sank back into contented reverie.

The Unbroken

"How are you going to write about the dark dimensions of aging? You obviously need to talk about pain, loneliness, and brokenness, for they are also a part of the elder years."

This was the question posed by my dear friend Natalie. We had done several writing retreats together where we shared our tender first thoughts and early writing, and then read our work aloud to each other. In the way of a good friend, she'd thrown down the gauntlet and challenged me to find ways to address the darker side of aging especially in this culture. Natalie was speaking from personal experience. She had lived with chronic pain for many years, a long struggle to avoid the series of operations that had disabled her mother. As for loneliness, although Natalie had a beautiful family, an exceptionally creative professional life, and of all my friends more lovers than any of them, even into her late seventies, yet still she longed for an enduring relationship that might assuage some of the loneliness that can come with living alone in the late years.

Faced with the enormity of these subjects and how they are woven through the experience of being an elder, I call upon the wisdom of the poets. Poetry can illuminate a profound subject with a few beautifully crafted words. The following poem is titled "The Unbroken." Read it once, twice, even three times, until it yields the depth of its vision to you.

There is a brokenness
  out of which comes the unbroken,
a shatteredness out of which blooms the unshatterable.
There is a sorrow
  beyond all grief which leads to joy
and a fragility out of whose depths emerges strength.
There is a hollow space too vast for words
  through which we pass with each loss,
out of whose darkness we are sanctioned into being.
There is a cry deeper than all sound
  whose serrated edges cut the heart
as we break open
to the place inside that is unbreakable and whole
  while learning to sing.[6]

These are the words of a contemporary mystic by the name of
Rashani Réa, a woman of vast talent—poet, musician, feminist,
grief whisperer, activist, ordained Buddhist, and still more—who
refers to her primary work as "engaged art." I've kept this poem
around for years. It has floated around my writing desk, disap-
pearing and then reappearing to remind me of a greater vision
that can hold even the most intolerable of sorrows. I felt the
poem asking to be included as part of this reflection on the sorrows of aging.

A Buddhist maxim says simply that pain is inevitable, but suffering is optional. This is one of those starkly stated truths about
life worthy of deep reflection. What kind of pain is it referring to?
All kinds—physical, emotional, existential, and spiritual pain, to
begin with. Whether the pain is propelled by physical causes as
in the case of chronic pain or illness, or by the emotional pain of
grief, depression, or despair, or by the emptiness of loss or loneliness, these states are all forms of the sorrow, shatteredness, and
brokenness about which Rashani's poem speaks.

We know that physical pain is a universal part of the human
condition, especially in the later years. Many elders start by re-

lying on medications to address physical symptoms, but sometimes even the best of modern medicine cannot alleviate the
persistence of chronic pain. Here's an imagined description of
intractable pain:

*Pain. The many faces of pain: piercing, unrelenting, lacerating,
burning, gnawing, throbbing, excruciating, unbearable. The adjec-
tives unfold with terrible ease.*

*Then the cascade of feelings that follow, feelings of descending into
the darkness, of neverending struggle. I am plummeting into another
realm, cut off from others, from the world, plunged into a world dominated by how to survive the next breath, the next hour, the next day.*

*The walls of life are closing in, obliterating everything else but how to
survive the next moment. Exiled into isolation and survival mode, this
is another reality with no resemblance to the life I've known.*

*Along with this descent and the heavy shadows of pain comes the
terrible dilemma of wanting to talk about what's happening, if I have
the energy, or if anyone is even willing to listen.*

*Now ruminations about life itself; how long can anyone tolerate
this level of pain? When will it break me in some cataclysmic episode?
How much life is enough?*

*Strategies unfold in irregular sequence. Keep lowering expecta-
tions. Upon reflection, there's no place for expectations at all. Hope
maybe, but even that is perilous territory. Expectations or hope may
end in disappointment and further discouragement. Neither of these
strategies will alleviate the pain of this situation, because both involve
the discrepancy between the reality of the moment and the wish for it
to be different.*

*I must give up trying to do anything. The greatest cause of this
suffering is the dissonance between my image of myself as healthy and
the reality of what's happening now.*

*Then a moment of insight. I can only go from moment to moment.
I have to give myself permission to let everything go, to surrender to
this initiation of pain. Ultimately this is about acceptance. Accept the
challenges of this situation. If not, I suffer. This insight begins to soften
the ruthless grip of mental struggle.*

With this subtle shift of perspective, an opening appears. Although it may be lost in the darkness of pain, the opening is always there, waiting. It doesn't necessarily mean the end of the pain, but an inner shift can allow for another perspective to soften the ragged edges of pain and sorrow. This is where the healing begins to happen.

In the words of Rashani's poem, the part of us that is unbroken, unshatterable, and beyond sorrow is there. This is the *spirit*, the light of consciousness, the pure awareness that is the essence of who we are. It is beyond the physical but still includes it. Spirit is the ultimate refuge that can hold the enormity of any experience, "that hollow space too vast for words...out of whose darkness we are sanctioned into being." Only those who have experienced the shift from the prison of pain to the freedom of release will understand how the heart's breaking—finally breaking open—reveals "the place inside that is unbreakable and whole."

Although it's easy to write about healing and spirit, in reality, when dealing with either physical or emotional suffering, the experience is never simple. It is overwhelming. Invariably, we ricochet between mental states, struggling to find some balance between being totally colonized by the suffering and progressively free of it. This is where the arresting, second part of the maxim comes in, "suffering is optional." The distinction is clearly made between the pain and our response to it, acknowledging the power of mind to work with the subtler emotional responses to pain and suffering.

The book *How To Be Sick* by Toni Bernhard is an inspiring example of how suffering might be optional. She contracted a basically incurable form of fatigue syndrome that left her severely handicapped, unable to work, needing to be cared for, the physically active part of her life brought to a standstill. When the book published, she'd already been ill for nine years. She learned what she calls the spiritual practice of "how to be sick," that is, how to live with joy and equanimity in spite of severe physical and energetic limitations. It's a moving account of her long and courageous struggle to find acceptance and compassion while dealing with an incurable disease.

A longtime Buddhist practitioner, Toni discovered many creative strategies for coping with serious illness, helpful to anyone regardless of spiritual orientation. Taking a lead from one of her teachers, she came up with the affirmation, "There is sickness here, but I am not sick."

This phrase and her contemplation of it were a powerful revelation and comfort. But she didn't stop there. She went on to contemplate, "Who is this 'I' who isn't sick?" Repeatedly posing the question "Who am I?" is an ancient spiritual practice that leads one to the Buddha's teaching on *anatta*, the premise that there is no solid self, no fixed, permanent identity that one can hold onto, an inquiry that appears in more detail later in this book.

Her revelation of being beyond the body and beyond the limited "I" is where the deep healing begins. This is the realm of pure awareness, of spirit, of infinite possibility, of freedom.

Whether with physical illness or emotional suffering, the enduring challenge is to bridge the discrepancy between the pain of this moment and our wish that it be different, or between our idealistic vision and the reality of how hard life is. Even His Holiness the Dalai Lama experiences this discrepancy.

At one of his annual three-day retreats in New York City, the Dalai Lama was lecturing about Manjushri, the archetype of wisdom in the Buddhist tradition. He explained that when we open to the experience of interconnectedness with the world, our sense of individuality softens and the heart opens with compassion toward all beings. This compassion has a radiance about it, he added. Suddenly he paused, interrupting his own train of thought.

"But that's not the way things are," he shared. "We are just people groping in the dark," and he put his head down and began to weep openly.

After a few moments, he sat up, blew his nose, and continued where he'd left off.

Even though the Dalai Lama was in the presence of thousands of people, this man, regarded as one of the world's greatest teachers, had exposed his humanness, his vulnerability, his grief. He had allowed the wave of grief to arise and wash through him, and then he went on, free of what had just happened.

So it can be for all of us. One moment, we aspire to the highest. The next moment, we're broken, collapsing helplessly into our vulnerability. In the face of great suffering—whatever form it takes, wherever it occurs—we need to bring great kindness and compassion to whatever arises. Maybe then, or eventually, we can experience the unbroken of Rashani's poem, the breaking open "...to the place inside that is unbreakable and whole/ While learning to sing."

The Dalai Lama's Story

I T WAS SPRING when the Dalai Lama came to New York City once again to offer teachings. About four thousand people were gathered in Radio City Music Hall, a surprising venue for such an event to take place. The stage had been transformed into a temple-like space, the backdrop covered with yards of softly hanging yellow silk and a large tangkha of Avalokiteshwara, the archetype of compassion. On either side of the Dalai Lama's raised chair were nearly one hundred monks and nuns, many having traveled from afar to be in the Dalai Lama's presence for the next three days.

He began with a story, one with special meaning for those of us who are in the later years. In the time of Shakyamuni Buddha, there lived an old man in his eighties who had done little about his spiritual life, and so he set out to find the Buddha's encampment. Looking like a beggar, bent with age and dressed in rags, he arrived at the encampment, tentatively approached one of the senior monks, and asked if he could be accepted into the *sangha*, the community of practitioners.

After testing the old man's attainment with a series of questions, the younger monk replied, "You are an old man and haven't done any practice, so there's no point in giving you teachings now."

Rejected and discouraged, the old man lay down in front of the door of the nearest shelter. Shortly after, the Buddha came by and asked him why he was lying there. The old man told of his rejection, to which the Buddha replied, "Some of my monks don't realize that just because the body is old, there's still every reason to practice. All you need is courage and enthusiasm to study and meditate. I know you have insight and the roots of virtue. I will care for you."

The Buddha blessed the old man, and, as the story goes, within a short time that old man became an *arhat*, a highly realized being.

As if to impress the point of the story, his Holiness added, "There's no reason to feel old just because the body is old. The mind can still be young and full of enthusiasm. We can have the courage to carry on our study and practice."

Two years later, the Dalai Lama, then in his seventy-ninth year, gave a public talk at the Boston Garden, where about 12,000 people were gathered. Although it was a secular setting and his entourage of monks and nuns were not there, the large tangkha of Avalokiteshvara hung once again behind his raised chair. As His Holiness slowly climbed the steps to the stage, he took off the Red Sox cap he'd been given for protection from the spotlights, waved it jauntily to the crowd, and then turned to face the tangkha. Immediately two attendants came to his side, supporting his elbows and holding him as he carefully made three prostrations, the traditional ritual of honoring a sacred image.

Many of us were struck by how much His Holiness had aged, and yet as he climbed the steps to his chair and began to speak, we instantly forgot the image of an old, frail man. His vibrant energy and resilient voice were that of a much younger man. He seemed an embodiment of the story that he had told a few years earlier.

PART II

WISDOM TREASURES

LIGHTING THE WAY:
INTRODUCTORY REFLECTIONS

A s I BEGAN to write this section of the book, quite unexpectedly the image of a stained glass window unfolded in my inner vision. Light shone through each piece of tempered glass—deep reds, blues, purples, and greens—rendering the window luminous and inexpressibly beautiful. As the image continued to unfold, it struck me that the lead, that held all the pieces in place, might symbolize the book's main themes: the call of the inner life, deepening in wisdom, and living consciously with the purpose of awakening—the spiritual dimensions of our lives.

In my late twenties, when I first started to practice meditation, I was an insatiable seeker, propelled by a deep longing to understand and eventually perhaps even experience what the wise ones had attained. What is it that propels Buddhist practitioners to do long meditation retreats, sometimes years in length? Many of the most eminent Tibetan masters spent twelve, fifteen, or even more years in solitary retreat and then emerged to become beacons of inspiration to practitioners worldwide.

What is enlightenment—the fully awakened mind/heart that leads almost inevitably to one becoming a widely known and respected teacher? The term "Christ consciousness" in the Christian tradition intrigued me, but I couldn't find the map for how to find one's way, something that is clearly laid out in the Buddhist tradition.

These were the kinds of questions that played around in my mind, vaguely in the background but with muted urgency. I continued to read voraciously, listen to teachings, and attend meditation retreats. Hob and I spent time with many eminent teachers, fortunate to be exposed to so much inspiration and wisdom. Particularly from the early days of exploring, I remember vivid moments when I'd stumble across some piece of wisdom that intrigued me. Some of these moments still shine with brightness.

To give an example, many years ago I happened upon a book that opened my eyes to another way of life. That morning I walked to the neighborhood Zen center only a block from our house. Frequently, Hob and I went to hear Seung Soeng, the Zen master whose playful and challenging teaching style, riddled with koans, had many of us tangled in perplexity and intrigued by the possibilities of the liberated mind.

In those days, I was still very much in beginner's mind, the sensitized, receptive state where even small discoveries can make a striking impact. That morning I happened to notice the galley of a manuscript sitting on a table in the hall, a surprise in itself as there were no books in that part of the center. As I began reading, I realized that the book was all about monastic life. It introduced the teachings about *samaya*, the vows by which monastics live, the relationship between teacher and student, and how the days were structured to support the process of awakening. Intrigued, I read on about the power of these vows to deepen commitment to practice and open the doors of awakening. Even though I had no aspirations to become a monastic, clearly many of the guidelines could apply to Hob and me as householders. I was especially struck by the idea that the kitchen could be the most compelling place for practice—a possibility that amazed me—for I was a young mother thoroughly on overload around the kitchen, the last place in the world, I thought, to offer a shred of inspiration!

Many of us are collectors of one thing or another—autographed books, bird lists, favorite stones, masks from other cultures, and so on. As a child, I began with wildflowers that I pressed and labeled, but somewhere in my thirties, I began collecting what I began to call wisdom treasures, bits of information to light the way through life. As the parent of a wild five-year-old and a toddler, I needed easy ways to remind myself of how to stay sane. I posted reminders on the refrigerator, put sayings on note cards for my bureau, even a sign that said "Breathe" on the dashboard of my car.

Over the years, my collection of wisdom treasures grew. Piles of notecards, entries in journals, quotations for talks. Quite simply, I love to be reminded of something inspiring. The possibilities are endless. The discoveries in the book about *samaya* inspired me to start.

Like the discoveries in the book about *samaya*, I started to keep a journal woven through with this and other pieces of wisdom. I copied the most compelling teachings I discovered onto notecards, then I put them in conspicuous places—my bureau, desk, kitchen counter, or meditation cushion—to serve as inspiration when I needed it. Some of these wisdom treasures appear in this section—a weaving of reflections, vignettes, stories, and practices. Some of them come from forty or more years ago, some more recent, each one like a part of that stained-glass window, illuminating some aspect of the dharma or spiritual life that stands out above all others.

THE SACRED CIRCLE

"Aging is not merely about the body losing its poise, strength,
and self-trust. Aging also invites you to become aware of the
sacred circle that shelters your life."
–JOHN O'DONOHUE, *Anam Cara*[7]

WHAT IS THE sacred circle that shelters your life? What
larger perspective, beyond the limited sense of self, creates meaning in your life? What ignites the flame of passion in
you? Where do you find inspiration to live your life more fully,
more expansively, more consciously?

The word "sacred" implies something that is hallowed or set
apart from the ordinary. Yet I had a wonderful friend, Alice
Howell, a prolific author and Jungian astrologer, who wrote with
inspiration and humor about finding the sacred in the commonplace. As one of the wayshowers who appears later in this book,
Alice elaborated on this theme in her treasure of a book entitled
The Dove in the Stone.

She writes about Iona, a small island off the island of Mull on
the west coast of Scotland that has been a place of pilgrimage for
thousands of years. Windswept and wild, a mystique surrounds
this island. Iona is often referred to as a power point on the earth's
surface, a phrase from geomancers who can sense the energies of
the land. Here one senses that there are realities beyond the ordinary. A sense of presence, of mystery, is embedded in the land
and in the island's history.

The land itself feels sacred, even to the unusual rocks found
on certain beaches. The most beloved beach is where St. Colum-
bo landed in the ninth century, where pilgrims go to collect the

smooth, variegated stones that seem to emanate a kind of holiness. Iona: a place where the veil between realities feels thin; where extra-ordinary things seem to happen like dream visions or images of ancestors or an unusual phenomenon like the mushrooms that emerge, after rain, to grow in perfect circles called fairy circles by the people of Iona.

In Iona, I discovered the sacred in the commonplace effortlessly. Like the deep, background tones in a piece of music, I experienced the mystery of this ancient island—the landscape, the sea, the crosses, the stone circle, the Abbey—all contributed to the sense that I was living in the midst of a sheltering, sacred circle. We can't, however, live our lives on pilgrimage to holy places. How then do we cultivate a sense of wonder and inspiration in our daily lives?

We know how easy it is to lapse into living on autopilot, moving through our days from to-do lists, slipping into habits that drain our energy and leave us wondering what happened to life's vividness. The pervasive presence of technology—email, iPhones, computers of every kind—may quietly colonize our lives, numbing us to the natural world and leaving us unaware of the addiction to being plugged in.

How do we stay awake to life? We will each find our own ways, but let me share seven guidelines that have struck me as indispensible to living consciously. They may seem simple, but the simple way is often the most powerful.

1) A spiritual orientation: As a dominant theme in my own life, I can affirm how my engagement with the inner life provides the sacred shelter of teachings and practices. It creates the framework that holds all of life's complexities and challenges; it serves as an inner compass, inviting ways to live with that orientation day by day, not just on the Sabbath. Oh yes, there are plenty of lapses and desert periods, but the compass needle finds true North again, leading back to trust in the knowledge that something beyond my limited self is providing both inspiration and shelter.

For many, this may not be their orientation, so for them the question is, what inspires you? What leads you on in your life? The answer will almost certainly include positive qualities such as generosity, kindness, patience, equanimity, compassion, and so on, which are regarded as expressions of the spiritual, the essence of living a noble life.

2) The practice of silence: Start the day with a period of quiet. It can be as short as a cup of tea or coffee by the window, not doing anything but simply *being*. Open to the new day. Appreciate relative good health. Feel gratitude for life's blessings.

Ideally, we may have some form of prayer, meditation, or inspirational reading—lectio divina—with which to begin the day. But this invitation to start quietly, gently, is to counterbalance the tendency to hurtle into action. More important, it's welcoming the blessing of another day.

3) The practice of mindfulness: When I first read *The Miracle of Mindfulness* by Thich Nhat Hanh back in the mid '70s, long before he became well-known, I made a sign and posted it on the refrigerator. In big block letters, each one a different color, it simply said "*mindfulness*," a reminder to bring one-pointed, sacred attention to ordinary activities like preparing food, cleaning up, walking from here to there, and so on. When we slow down and go through our activities with full attention, it's astonishing how wondrous the simplest things are! Look at your hands and appreciate the extraordinary job they do—constantly—yet how often do we pay them any attention at all?

4) The practice of stopping: When I remember, I break into the momentum of my day by periodically stopping. Otherwise it's too easy to miss some of life's most precious moments: the flash of light in a raindrop hanging on a leaf, the joy in a child's face, the tenderness in an old person's eyes, an extraordinary cloud formation in the sky.

By stopping, we interrupt the mindless momentum that dominates our lives. Become aware of the breath's gentle movement, especially during routine activities. Stopping can be a form of prayer. We open to a timeless moment. We appreciate the wonder of being alive. We experience life through all of our senses and feel thankful for this moment.

5) Finding the sacred in the commonplace: This guideline follows from the previous one; we have to stop in order to experience the sacred. For me, a sense of wonder is synonymous with the word sacred. How about the iridescence on a flower petal? Or the cup whose emptiness allows you to savor your tea. Or synchronicities as when your friend calls the moment you're thinking about them. Or simply the silence that offers respite from a noisy world.

Life offers us a steady stream of small wonders, yet we're often not at home, not present with ourselves to experience them.

6) Meditative moments: Another practice, part of stopping, is to sit back, close your eyes, and just be for a few moments. Bring awareness to the body, appreciate its rhythm, how it brings life to the body. Invite the mind to let go of thoughts, soften, and become as spacious as a vast sky. Just rest in being, the mind quiet.

7) The practice of gratitude: Gratitude is a movement of the heart, a pause in the usual stream of life where we feel or say thank you for a kindness, a gift given, or for an unexpected moment that brings joy. We are surprised by joy, for gratitude is woven with joy even if the connection is subtle.

Gratitude may feel like a gentle rush of energy, fullness in the heart, the softening of personal boundaries. With gratitude, there's a sense of momentary wholeness. The words "whole" and "holy" are related, thus bestowing gratitude with a sense of the sacred. The medieval mystic Meister Eckhart said that if our only prayer was "thank you," that was sufficient.

Returning to the image of the sacred circle that can shelter our life, these guidelines can help to point the way to that experience. These are some of mine, but each of us will discover our own. As I see it, the invitation is how to live consciously, age gracefully, and open to the mystery in which we live.

Even with these guidelines, the real test comes when life cat-apults everything we've known into uncertainty. What perspec-tives hold our life in balance during tumultuous times? Where is our sacred circle then, or—to use another image—what might our ultimate refuge be? For each of us the answer will be dif-ferent. In the following vignette, I was taken totally by surprise when confronted with this very issue at a tender time.

Know Your Refuges

UNLESS THEY'VE HAD the experience, no one knows how exhausting it is to be the caregiver of someone with Alzheimer's. When Hob was in the middle stages of the illness, I sometimes felt as though we were flying off the tracks of some crazy roller coaster. The heartbreaking surprises mounted daily. Worn out and weary, I finally found someone to provide respite care so I could attend a few days at a meditation retreat.

During the retreat, we were assigned a ten-minute meeting with one of the dharma teachers to discuss how our practice was going. My account was filled with flashbacks to frustrating situations, about how to handle anger and heartbreak, and the morning-to-night demands of caring for someone with dementia. At the edge of tears, I stopped. The teacher responded quietly, her voice the embodiment of compassion.

"Do you know your refuges, Olivia?"

I was momentarily taken aback. I hadn't thought about refuges in relationship to my situation. I knew the tradition of taking refuge in the Buddha, dharma, and *sangha*—one's potential for awakening, appreciation of the teachings, and support by the spiritual community.

Her simple question triggered a lot of subsequent reflection in relation to my current situation as weary caregiver, and to everyone's life in general. Taking refuge—an inspiring practice—has its equivalent in all spiritual traditions. In Christianity, one takes refuge in Jesus or Christ consciousness, the all-loving wisdom that the historical Jesus embodied. To take refuge in the dharma of Christianity would mean the truth of the teachings. The sangha in Christianity is the church as well as the community that provides inspiration and support, including the wise ones who followed Jesus's path.

Refuge. The concept kept working on me. I discovered I could take refuge in the present moment. Such an obvious, simple idea, much emphasized by Thich Nhat Hanh. I remember the moment when it first struck me not as an abstract idea but as a living reality. The present—the only place where life happens.

The breath is yet another refuge. I hadn't connected the two words—breath and refuge—until many years ago when I was a speaker at the first large training conference in Behavioral Medicine. Although my work had always involved public speaking, something about being the first conference of its kind plus all the medical professionals from around the world stirred up an unusual bout of nervousness. I could feel my heart pounding, my breath shortening, my mouth going dry as if I were chewing on cotton. Plain and simple, I was scaring myself!

Then—oh so obvious—I remembered the breath. How many tens of thousands of times had I done this in meditation or at other times, but totally forgot when I most needed it. Very consciously, I took refuge in the rising and falling of each breath. My attention turned within to deepening the breath, rather than being eclipsed by an outward focus that had triggered the anxiety. My heart rate slowed, my mouth moistened, and my breath deepened into the slow, steady rhythm that allows one to come home again, free from the whirl of self-created anxiety. Such a gift. The supreme irony of this situation was that I was giving a talk about the role of breath and the power of meditation to quiet the nervous system!

Over time, meditation becomes another refuge. As one abides—even if only occasionally—in states of absorption where the discursive mind has quieted down and thoughts seem faint or nonexistent, one experiences a vast field of awareness, spacious and full of boundless potential. One might say that this experience—subtle beyond words—is the ultimate refuge.

Finding refuge—a simple practice, yet profound in its support. Perhaps you haven't given much thought to the subject, or wonder what your source of refuge might be. The possibilities are endless: a short prayer, a mantra, Jesus, Buddha, Mohammed, a spiritual teacher, music (as it was for a conductor friend of mine), a short teaching, a poetic fragment, and on and on. Whatever brings you back to yourself.

A beautiful example of refuge occurred when I was a Hospice volunteer for a woman who was dying of cancer. She wanted all of us to know that her refuge mantra was, "Thy will be done." Her four sons would take turns sitting by her bed, quietly reciting the prayer on each outbreath, and over the next few days helped her ease into a peaceful death. Her refuge became everyone's refuge. By sharing her refuge prayer, she helped to transform the last days of her life not only for herself but for her entire family.

For sure, to have a sense of an inner refuge becomes more important as we age. It is yet another way of preparing ourselves for the unknown challenges that lie ahead. Sometimes refuge takes the form of a strongly held perspective that can ease even the greatest challenges. As the next vignette illustrates, that was true for a dear friend who had lost her sight.

A JEWEL OF WISDOM

PRICELESS TIDBITS OF wisdom are hidden—or sometimes not so hidden—in the ordinary moments of our lives. One of my treasures came from a dear elder friend named Blanche who had been gradually losing her sight to glaucoma. As she lived in California, I only saw her intermittently, but now in her early nineties, she had finally lost all sight. One doesn't wait around to visit friends in their nineties, so I arranged a trip with the intention of seeing her before it was too late.

Of delicate stature but emanating inner strength, she was sitting in her favorite armchair with her back to the window. Her white hair was drawn back into a bun with errant strands around her face. Dark glasses protected her eyes, which I remembered as being brilliant blue. After some preliminary catching up, I asked her about the final loss of sight and how she was handling the challenges of her daily life. As was her way, she paused for a moment, tilted her head a little as if listening deep within, and replied quietly, "I try to treat every moment as new experience."

An extraordinary statement—a jewel of wisdom that describes the essence of mindfulness. *Every moment as new experience.* Her words were an heroic response to an overwhelming life change. Countless times those words, along with her assured presence, have come flying back to rescue me from some distracted, fragmented state. She gave me a timeless wisdom treasure.

Blanche was a wisdom figure in her own right. A writer, poet, and seeker of the truth, many friends sought out her company, including well-known figures like Alan Watts and Krishnamurti. My visits with her felt like a form of pilgrimage. Our conversations ranged across a variety of fields but most often dwelled on philosophical questions, religion, psychology, and the new therapies in which I was then training. I don't remember her identifying herself with any particular tradition, but she delighted in any conversation that touched on deepening one's inner life or matters of the heart.

Practices of the Heart

Many years ago, *in northern India: The rainy season is approaching. The Buddha and his monks are staying at a monastery. As the season is changing and monsoon clouds are gathering over the towering Himalayas, they are preparing for the rain's retreat, traditionally a time for an extended period of meditation practice.*

One day during their preparations, a group of the monks approach the Buddha and ask if they can spend the retreat in a distant forest. They receive his permission, and they set forth on their journey and find their way into the forest. Each monk finds shelter under a big tree as a temporary residence and begins his practice.

Meanwhile, the local deities are annoyed by this incursion of monks. Not only is their intention to stay for more than three months, but the spiritual power of their meditation has driven the deities from their tree-abodes, forcing them to live on the ground. So the deities set about to harass the monks in all sorts of ways, especially frightening them as they practice at night.

Exasperated by the situation, the monks go back to the Buddha and explain what has happened. The Buddha responds with a teaching, his first teaching on loving-kindness known as the Metta sutta. He suggests that they recite the verses from his teaching and send the power of their love to all beings everywhere, especially to the angry deities who have been driven from their abodes in the tree canopy.

Inspired by the teaching, the monks return to the forest and begin to practice metta, sending the radiance of love to the deities and in all directions. The deities are pleased by all the loving energy coming their way, and so they leave the monks alone, free to practice without any further harassment.

This story appears in a classic Buddhist text, giving us the origin of the much-loved practice of *metta* or loving-kindness. Metta is a Pali word that is difficult to translate but which connotes "friendliness." The word suggests that we become not only a friend to ourselves but to everyone, to all beings—as the phrase goes—whether we know them or not. This practice calls us to experience unconditional love, an open-heartedness that starts with ourselves and extends out to all, including those toward whom we may feel neutral or even averse. It is a profound practice that can become a path in and of itself.

To illustrate the depths of love that are possible, the Buddha chose the image of a mother's love for her only child to convey such total dedication to the wellbeing of another. As a favorite section of the sutra says:

> Even as a mother protects with her life
> Her child, her only child,
> So with a boundless heart
> Should one cherish all living beings;
> Radiating kindness over the entire world....

When I first heard this story, I was struck not only by the whimsical struggle between the forest deities and the monks, but by a practice that included an element of protection. Protection from what? The forest deities symbolize the familiar tendencies of our minds to get lost in distraction, fantasy, worry, and fear, or in other words to get caught yet again in cycles of self-absorption, relating to life through the narrow lens of ego/self—the primary source of our suffering.

As Shantideva, the renowned sage of ninth century India, wrote in *The Way of the Bodhisattva,*

> Whatever joy there is in this world
> All comes from desiring others to be happy,
> And whatever suffering there is in this world,
> All comes from desiring myself to be happy.[8]

Yet in the story of the monks and the tree deities, the Buddha's invitation to practice metta suggests that protection was needed not only from outer conditions, like people or other beings who harass and frighten you, but from inner conditions of our own mind that can create equally troubling and fearful scenarios. It's a beautiful, compassionate way to deal not only with oneself but with our relationship to others.

The practice of metta starts with an invitation to open the heart, first to ourselves. We begin by sending kindness to ourselves, because before we can send loving-kindness to others, we must first experience it for ourselves. Almost like blessing ourselves, we repeat silently whatever favorite phrases truly touch us: May I be happy. May I be free from suffering. May I be free from harm. May I have ease of heart. May I be calm and at ease. May I be peaceful.

These are traditional phrases, but most important is to find the phrases that resonate with you. Once they become natural and internalized, they're like the blessing of a gentle spring rain that brings a sense of calm and wellbeing.

Then we reset the compass of our attention on others. As a practice of the heart, sending loving-kindness to others is propelled by the intentionality of an awakened heart. Visualizing the person or calling them by name, "May you be happy. May you be free from suffering," and so forth.

In this shortened version of loving-kindness practice, finally we extend the wish of loving-kindness to all beings. "May all beings be happy; may all beings be peaceful," and so on.

Practices that involve some form of blessing or wishing others well are common to many spiritual traditions. There is the practice of blessing from the Christian tradition; not the automatic, dry recitations one sometimes hears, but a blessing that truly carries the energy of the heart—a loving intention turned outward toward a certain person that they may be well and happy, free from harm and sorrow, and abide in equanimity and peace—a blessing sent as prayer or thought or visualization.

From the Tibetan tradition, there is the practice of *tonglen*—the exchange of self and other—a powerful practice where you breathe in the suffering and sorrows of others into the space of the heart, so vast and spacious it can hold all suffering, and let the dark energy transform into positive qualities, like kindness, generosity, patience, and compassion that you breathe out and convey to the other.

His Holiness the Dalai Lama has provided an inspiring example of this practice. Reporters often ask him for his views about the Chinese, given the horrors they have perpetrated on the Tibetan people. He answers with the simple statement, "I take on the pain of the Chinese and give them my happiness." His statement takes my breath away. It illustrates how a situation can be transformed no matter how harrowing and extreme the circumstances may be. As someone has said, love and compassion are not nouns; they are verbs, an exchange of energy between people.

I remember experiencing an "aha" when I saw how metta, tonglen, and blessing practices are all facets of the same jewel—all share deep empathy toward others, all wish to cultivate love in action. These images for sending blessings are based on the interdependence of all beings everywhere, across time and space, and based on the principles of quantum physics and consciousness theory. Certainly these are vast fields, yet here consciousness is posited as the foundation of all things animate and inanimate, so that all our thoughts and actions have an impact, however subtle, on the web of consciousness that connects everyone, everywhere, encircling the entire planet.

These practices of the heart share a liberating quality. They turn the compass from self-concern to caring for others. They awaken the heart/mind so that we see everyone as worthy of our love and acceptance. They can manifest anywhere, anytime—toward the checkout person, fellow worker, homeless woman, sick friend, family member—with the simple wish for their wellbeing. This practice of quiet blessing can become woven through one's life, softening and opening the heart. Gradually it creates a force field of compassion that knows no bounds.

The Moments Between

As someone trying to live consciously, I'm surprised by how often I find myself lost in interludes of total distraction. I drift along in some completely useless sea of thought, lost in musings and imaginings, totally out of touch with the reality right before me. I think of it as living *beside* life, instead of in the immediacy of the moment.

Why does that matter? you might wonder. Life only happens in the present moment. Obvious, you say, but how often do we get lost in thought without ever being aware of it. In Buddhism, the inference is that every moment of distraction is a moment of life lost. Or, to put it another way, every moment of mindfulness is another step on the path to awakening.

I began to notice how that drifting happens most often while between activities—coming and going from the house, going up and down stairs, walking from here to there, and so on. How often one activity—sometimes a major event—follows one after another in rapid succession with no time to process or integrate what I have just experienced. Does this sound at all familiar?

Acknowledging this pattern, the French have an expression to mark arrivals and departures in one's daily life. "*Rite d'arrivé*" and "*rite de sortie.*" They acknowledge that moments of coming and going are important, and that we shouldn't rush through them; rather we need to pause and take a few moments—preferably more—to appreciate these transitions.

Because I often experience the headlong momentum of my life, this small, honoring ritual stuck in my memory. Doorways or thresholds are a particularly interesting place to watch. No wonder in the Jewish tradition there is the custom of putting a *mezuzah*—a prayer on a little parchment scroll—on the door frame as a reminder of the sacred amidst one's comings and goings.

We can't live in today's world without feeling the accelerating pace of life, propelled ever faster by technology, media, instant messaging, and so on. With this steady barrage and the apparent need to be connected to some device for much of a day, it's no wonder our minds spin out of control, lost in thousands of details, demands, and distractions.

Especially as elders, we have the choice to step out of the fast-paced culture we live in, and one way is to slow down and acknowledge transitions. I know that's why this simple reminder—*rite d'arrivé* and *rite de sortie*—caught my attention.

A gradual slowing down is a natural part of the aging process. It is a gift, often received with a sense of relief, even delight. With this gift, we may become more aware of the quality of our lives—the rhythm of the day and a sense of balance that might have eluded us in the hurly burly of the workplace.

WITH SOFTNESS AND EASE

IT IS A *raw, March day in the early '70s when Munindra-ji, a well-known Bengali monk, comes to speak at our local meditation center. We're looking forward to being with this monk who has been an inspiration to some of the early Western Buddhist teachers and their students.*

After his talk, a few of us including Munindra-ji gather for tea in our friend's kitchen. There is a flurry of activity as we all get our tea, the sound of the boiling kettle, the snatches of friends talking, the click of spoons against cups, the jostle of chairs as we settle around the kitchen table for conversation.

Munindra-ji sits quietly, saying little. Slight of stature, dressed in white, he strikes me as an unusual combination of gentleness and power, his eyes steady and penetrating. When the conversation turns to how to integrate meditation with our daily lives, at one moment he turns toward me, makes strong eye contact and says quietly, "Always do everything with softness and ease."

Such simple words yet they strike me with force. They are clearly directed at me; how well I know my recurring pattern of pushing through tasks, feeling pressured, and accelerating into a fast forward mode that feels out of balance.

These words—"do everything with softness and ease"—are a reminder to slow down, be gentle and fully present—meditation in action. Such a simple, powerful message, especially for today's world with its accelerating pace of life and proliferating, time-pressured demands.

Munimdra-ji's message has resurfaced countless times over the years. Reflect on how often it happens that some message—spoken or read—drops into your unconscious and then surfaces much later when a situation calls for it. There it is: helpful guidance, a wisdom treasure. It's almost like alchemy; as in the symbolism of base metal transforming into gold, something apparently ordinary becomes something precious.

WHO ARE YOU NOW?

"WHO AM I?" The eternal question. I've heard this question raised, often with some surprise, while teaching elder groups and in the two circles of which I'm a part, one the Self-ordination Circle, the other focused on aging and end-of-life issues. As urgent as this question might have been when we were adolescents or young adults, it may resurface in the later years when our identities are less formed around jobs, careers, and family. Now it has another kind of urgency. The question seems to penetrate deeper; the inner terrain feels as though it's changed, our perspectives shifted. Depending on issues of energy and health, we're now very aware that the largest part of our life is behind us, that unknowns lie ahead, and that the ultimate mystery—death—waits at the far end of time.

The answer to this question takes different forms as we move through life. It forms our personal narrative, always changing. These responses add up to our life story. As we become elders, the question may involve different nuances. To give a significant example, if we have a contemplative practice, the solidified sense of "I" has begun to erode. Former ways of identifying ourselves, particularly the roles we've played, have lost their importance, even disappeared.

"Who am I?" is a specific meditation practice. I've encountered it both in training with a Korean Zen master and in the Hindu tradition of Ramana Maharshi, one of the sages of modern India. One holds the question "Who am I?" in awareness, not seeking an answer but rather as an opening into pure awareness, free of any description. It's an invitation for the mind to let go of its habitual tendencies to cognize, analyze, compare, and spin endless scenarios. For the question "Who am I?" is unanswerable. There is no one identity that consolidates into the concept of "I." This is deeply unsettling for those who are attached to the various identities that comprise what they think of as their "personality."

This challenging idea is at the heart of Buddhist practice. *Anatta* is the Pali word that translates loosely as "no self" or empty of a separate self. If you look into the constituents of the "self," we are composed of an infinite complexity of parts that are interwoven with life around us—past, present, and future. We exist because of the mother who gave us birth, all those who cared for us, taught us, hired us, related to us, and so forth. We exist because of the food we eat, the air we breathe, the water we drink; without which we could not live. Furthermore, we're conditioned by everything that happens to us, a moment-to-moment process of which we're largely unaware. Each experience tempers us in subtle ways. We are in a constant process of change. Finally, we come to the conclusion that the "self" doesn't exist as a separate entity but as a complex aggregation of interconnected parts.

Obviously, we all carry some kind of image of who we are—the seemingly continuous aspects of our personality that we think of as our "self." We need this concept—for that is all it is—not only to negotiate the world but because it provides us with some sense of identity.

There's a powerful secret hidden here. One of the mysteries of aging is that the combination of our accrued years, our life experience, and our expanded sense of our place in the world softens this sense of "I." It's huge relief! I now experience softer ego boundaries, deeper connection to those around me and to the world at large, enhanced freedom from the expectations and opinions of others, and overall a greater sense of freedom from self-preoccupation.

As Einstein wrote, "The true value of a human being is determined primarily by the measure and the sense in which he (she) has attained liberation from the self."[9]

Some might argue that, on the contrary, their sense of themselves is stronger than ever in the later years. After all, they've spent a lifetime solidifying their sense of self through family, friends, work, and so forth.

What a contrast then to learn about a Native American tribe in the Northwest whose language has no first person pronoun, no word for "I." When someone asks them who they are, they reply by describing who they are related to; for example, the daughter of so-and-so, the sister of so-and-so, mother, cousin, aunt of so-and-so, etc. Along with those to whom they are related, their collective identity is what matters, in contrast to the primacy of the individual "I" so embedded in our culture.

When Desmond Tutu came to speak at Harvard Divinity School, he also talked about how his people in South Africa don't think in terms of the personal "I." If you ask someone how they are, instead of answering, "I'm fine," as most Americans would do, the person might answer, "We're not well as my mother-in-law is suffering with cancer." As long as someone in their family circle isn't well, they aren't well either, a testament to the strength of the communal ethic in their culture.

In any state of absorption, whether meditation or an activity we love, the sense of self dissolves into pure awareness. How does this relate to our aging? In a deep and wonderful way: we begin to sense something boundless and supremely free, far beyond the limiting sense of a separate self. In Eastern traditions, this is called awakening or liberation—or at least a taste of liberation. The experience may come occasionally or for brief moments, but once experienced, it's a promise of the ultimate freedom, and never forgotten. We've glimpsed the truth that we are far more than the limited self we think we are. These glimpses are like a golden thread that leads us onward into further practice, insight, and freedom.

Who are you now? There is no one answer. What freedom! And beautifully expressed in one of my favorite of Rilke's poems.

I live my life in widening circles
that reach out across the world.
I may not complete this last one
but I give myself to it.

I circle around God, around the primordial tower.
I've been circling for thousands of years
and I still don't know; am I a falcon,
a storm, or a great song?[10]

We may recognize the mysteries of identity expressed in the poem. Or we may have experienced intimations of freedom from self-cherishing, but as we all know, the aging process can also be ruthless as when one's sense of identity gradually dissolves into dementia. That experience varies dramatically from person to person, but the next story is inspiring in how an elderly gentleman continued to see the essence of his beloved quite apart from her apparent loss of identity.

How to Dance in the Rain

(Note: Years ago, the following story was sent to me by a friend. Since there was no attribution, I want to thank the author for this inspiring piece.)

I T WAS A busy morning, about 8:30, when an elderly gentleman in his eighties arrived to have stitches removed from his thumb. He said he was in a hurry as he had an appointment at 9:00 am.

I took his vital signs and had him sit down, knowing it would be over an hour before someone would to able to see him. I saw him looking at his watch and decided, since I was not busy with another patient, I would evaluate his wound. On exam, it was well healed, so I talked to one of the doctors, got the needed supplies to remove his sutures and redress his wound.

While taking care of his wound, I asked if he had another doctor's appointment this morning, as he was in such a hurry. The gentleman told me no, that he needed to go to the nursing home to eat breakfast with his wife. I inquired as to her health.

He told me that she had been there for a while and that she was a victim of Alzheimer's disease. As we talked, I asked if she would be upset if he was a bit late.

He replied that she no longer knew who he was, that she had not recognized him in five years now. I was surprised, and asked him, "And you still go every morning, even though she doesn't know who you are?"

He smiled as he patted my hand and said, "She doesn't know me, but I still know who she is."

I had to hold back tears as he left, I had goose bumps on my arm, and thought, "That is the kind of love I want in my life."

True love is neither physical, nor romantic. True love is an acceptance of all that is, has been, will be, and will not be.

The happiest people don't necessarily have the best of everything; they just make the best of everything they have....

Life isn't about how to survive the storm, but how to dance in the rain.

A JOYFUL MIND

IT WAS A memorable meeting. I'd been told about Leonard before I met him, though I had no idea that he would become such an important person in my life. He'd lived in an ashram for five years, some of that time in India where I'd also visited. Everybody loved him and spoke of him as their special friend. He was devoted to this spiritual tradition where devotees sometimes asked for spiritual names. He'd been given the name Mahadev, a form of the divine in Hinduism.

The morning we met, Mahadev was sitting by himself at a table in the corner of a large dining room where he was peeling piles of garlic in preparation for the noonday meal. He was in a wheelchair, something no one had mentioned, because that seemed to have little to do with who he was. I learned that he had muscular dystrophy, a ruthless, degenerative disease that had been diagnosed in his childhood. By his late teens, no longer able to walk, he was confined to a wheelchair. He was now slightly bent over, his bearded face intent on this humblest of tasks.

As I walked over to introduce myself, he looked up, greeted me with a warm smile, and invited me to sit down. I picked up a piece of garlic and joined in peeling. I noticed his very limited physical movements, how he needed one arm to lift the opposite hand, and how immobilized the rest of his body seemed to be. Yet his face—the most animated part of him—radiated warmth. The depth of his loving attention was easy, all embracing, altogether magnetizing. He was one of those memorable people with whom I felt an immediate bond, as though we'd known each other forever.

Over many years of cherished friendship, I marveled at how he handled almost total physical limitation. He lived with the help of a personal attendant and accepted the help that people willingly offered, because he was like a magnet that drew people to him. People were invariably clustered around his wheelchair, drawn by his loving nature and the quiet joy he emanated.

Several years after we first met, four of us, including his attendant and my daughter Laura, decided to go on pilgrimage to some of the sacred sites in rural India. We were faced with the seemingly insurmountable challenges of traveling with Mahadev, yet ambitious as our plan was, he reassured us that we could do it, that help always seemed to arrive when he needed it.

We discovered this from the moment of our departure in the pre-dawn dark. I don't know where they came from, but as the bus slowed to a stop, several men appeared out of the darkness to help lift his body onto the bus. That happened with each major move of our journey. People always appeared to help us through difficult situations.

Traveling through rural India with Mahadev was one of the most memorable parts of the pilgrimage. Laboriously, we pushed his wheelchair over bumpy, unpaved pathways, carried him up temple steps, and even once found four strangers who offered to carry him on a palanquin into a remote temple complex. Through all this, Mahadev somehow conveyed his gratitude and warm-heartedness even though there was no shared language with those who helped. Wherever we went, we watched with wonder as crowds gathered around him. The people of rural India had never seen a wheelchair. Maybe equally unusual was someone who sought to connect with them, who radiated such warmth and joy. Mahadev never showed the slightest impatience or dismay over his disability. It was his inner state that drew people to him. In spite of monumental challenges, Mahadev lived with remarkable equanimity and joy. His life was an inspiration.

These reminiscences bring to mind how life gives us the messages we need, whether we heed them at the time or not. In retrospect, I came to realize what an inspiring influence Mahadev had had on my life. His equanimity and joy were a teaching without words. Undoubtedly he had his dark moments like any of us, but mostly his warm, steady presence in the face of his adversity affirmed what a strong mind and heart he had.

What a contrast to the afflictive thoughts that can invade our minds—fear, anger, worry, anxiety, depression—all varieties of emotional turbulence. These reminiscences about Mahadev led me to reflect on how we can transform our afflictive patterns. Several teachings come to mind, each one inspiring.

The first offers a way to interrupt the momentum of negativity. The moment you recognize that you're entangled in some strong emotion, ask yourself what is called "a vertical question," one that breaks into the continuity of thoughts and startles you into a new perspective. In the midst of your worrying, for example, you might ask, "Where is happiness in this moment?"

When I first heard this suggestion, I remember bridling inwardly. "That's too much to ask!" It was the rebel in me protesting what I initially thought was an impossibly idealistic teaching. Nevertheless, I continued to ponder the slogan, figuring that some early Buddhist teacher had put this out as an aspiration. Aspiration, or acting "as if" some positive outcome is possible, is very much a part of the tradition, so maybe I could give this idea a chance by broadening the meanings of happiness. Surely it was possible, for example, to have equanimity in the face of a difficult situation, as Mahadev consistently proved. Just thinking about equanimity invites a shift in feeling, the sense that all is well, whatever is happening on the outside. The thought of equanimity triggers other words like serenity, wellbeing, acceptance, or any positive quality that might counteract a difficult feeling.

I was intrigued by this idea of asking a vertical question and played with it, noticing especially those in-between moments when I felt a slight sinking mood or a shadow of foreboding about something in my life. I'd conjure up a phrase, and almost instantly I'd notice a slight shift of energy, enough to end the sinking spell and bring a measure of contentment. Remembering the phrase tipped me toward gratitude. I'd appreciate how in reality all was well, and that the blessings in my life far outweighed some momentary mood.

I recognized how that wily trickster of the mind was creating a problem where there didn't need to be one. I thought of this practice as "turning the moment around," another way to describe this strategy: notice your negative thinking and intentionally interrupt it.

A similar idea appears in the Lojong sayings, fifty-nine short mind-training exercises from the Tibetan tradition. "Always keep a joyful mind" is one of the favorite aphorisms. Composed by a twelfth century master, these aphorisms aim at refining the mind by counteracting negative mind habits that color our moods and drive our actions. They are often only a few words in length—decisive and memorable—easy to remember for those who heard them from the days when most people didn't read. The aphorisms also include methods for cultivating positive qualities like kindness, compassion, and an expanded vision of the world.

I heard yet another version of this teaching that took the aspiration of a joyful mind even further. Tsoknyi Rinpoche, a Tibetan who teaches regularly in the West, had his own phrase, "happiness for no reason," a thought-provoking slogan and something of a surprise, especially in our materialistic culture where happiness is so often promised with aggressive marketing and objects to be bought. This was an invitation to rest in a natural state of mind that was free of dependence on outer circumstances, an ultimate form of freedom.

"Where is happiness in this moment?"

"Always keep a joyful mind."

"Happiness for no reason."

These are all wisdom treasures—three versions of a powerful teaching.

Why should one care about these mind states and their impact? Buddhist teachings always make clear that we do these practices in mind training and meditation not for ourselves alone but for the benefit of all—an exalted perspective, but one based on the truth that we live in an infinitely interconnected world. As the wise ones say, everything we think, say, or do matters in the larger context of which we're all a part. Mahadev's life exemplified this truth; his joy touched countless lives, an inspiration to many.

Compassion for Yourself

I T IS QUITE common that we are kinder and more compassionate toward others than we are toward ourselves. This may be especially true for those of us in the helping professions, where our attention is weighted toward concern for others while forgetting to treat ourselves with the same acceptance and kindness. The following excerpt from the *Tao Te Ching* by Lao-Tsu jumped out at me, because at the time I first encountered it, I particularly needed the wisdom in the last sentence.

> I have just three things to teach:
> Simplicity, patience, compassion.
> These three are your greatest treasures.
> Simple in actions and in thoughts,
> you return to the source of being.
> Patient with both friends and enemies,
> you accord with the way things are.
> Compassionate toward yourself,
> you reconcile all beings in the world.

If you contemplate just this one passage, that could suffice for getting along in our troubled world. Those words are inspirational, but what do we do when our lives feel fraught with impossible challenges, like so many of the times when I felt overwhelmed during Hob's illness with Alzheimer's?

※

It's another day in an endless succession of days dominated by caregiving.

Hob's probably in the late middle stages of the disease, at least that's how I'm framing it these days.

Occasionally he talks about his disease. As he's told me before, he thinks he's approaching the point when "it's time for me to get off the bus." That's his casual way of talking about dying. He's determined not to live into the late stages, because he has seen what happened with my mother who had also had Alzheimer's. But how do you do that? He's talked about options. We've talked together about options. He says he will stop eating.

My mind wanders into perilous territory. What's my role is this? How does anyone decide when? Will he ask me to help him? What's my responsibility—to support him or buy more time? I can feel myself sinking into a morass of heavy feelings.

I'm exhausted from the strains of living for two people. I'm his eyes so he won't fall when we're out walking. I'm his ears when he doesn't understand what someone says. I'm his word finder, guessing at what he's trying to express. I'm taking over from the mind he's losing—remembering names, retrieving lost stories, juggling the parts of his life that remain. I'm exhausted and heartbroken. I wonder how long I can go on. I know he feels isolated by his illness, and so do I. How can anyone possibly imagine what this is like unless they've been through it?

I'm aware of the heavy, whirling tangle of feelings, but what to do about it? I'm struggling between the heaviness and longing for some lightness. Then I think about Hob and what he's going through, and that sparks a glimmer of compassion. A shift from my self-concerns to his suffering. How remarkable that he often brings lightness to his situation. This moment of recognition brings more compassion for him, then finally for myself too.

It takes a while, but slowly I remember a simple exercise I've shared in groups—the practice of having compassion for oneself. It starts with remembering the body. I put my left hand over my heart center and bring awareness to my breath. "*Slow down.... deepen.... calm....*" I say to myself. I feel the focus on my breath beginning to eclipse the power of my wild thinking.

I start to repeat silently some of the phrases,

"May I have compassion for myself....
May I find acceptance....
May my heart be at ease....
May I have compassion for myself...."

The phrases are like a soothing litany, softening the hard edges of my mental anguish.

Only when I feel some compassion toward myself can I fully extend it back to him. *"We're in this together. We both need compassion."*

I start extending the phrases to Hob. And beyond. Everyone needs compassion. I remember the phrase that makes the wish universal: *"May I have compassion for all beings."*

This one small moment as a caregiver reveals a larger truth; we start with our own need for compassion, then focus our compassion to the one we're with, and finally to all beings. In the process, my preoccupation with my situation dissolves into the universal wish for all to experience compassion. This weaves me back into a larger whole—the world family of all those struggling with challenges of every kind.

Somehow one small wisdom treasure can lead us where we need to go, lightening the burden of whatever we were carrying. Far too often we find ourselves carrying burdens of worry or preoccupied with karmic entanglements. How they stubbornly persist! That was my situation when, quite by chance, I discovered an important bit of wisdom in the dharma book I was then reading. It gave me another view. "View" is a key word, an overarching perspective that provides direction and inspiration for one's practice. As often happens, some teaching comes along at just the moment we need it, as happened with the vignette that follows.

Pure Perception

I WAS WALKING along a remote country road in northern Vermont during a retreat at a friend's house. After a quiet morning reading Buddhist teachings, I set out walking south, where at one point the fields give way to dense forest. By now, I knew this road, and each time I came to that place, I felt the shift from one realm to another. The roadway darkened, the air cooled, and the hemlocks obscured the sun. This sheltered part of the walk always seemed mysterious.

That morning, in the shadowed light, I experienced the shift in a compelling way. My rambling thoughts suddenly ceased. My mind went into neutral and produced one of those flashes of possibility that arise when the mind is not grasping at past or future, nor trying to think something through. Seemingly out of nowhere arose a Tibetan phrase I'd been musing over just hours earlier: *tag-nang*. It means "pure perception" or "sacred outlook." The moment I read the word, I felt its power and knew it could lead through the thickets of samsaric life to the freedom of enlightenment. I felt as though the phrase was knocking at the door of awareness, asking for recognition.

The phrase continued to play in my mind for a few moments. Then, like shifting lenses, I was suddenly totally awake, seeing everything with vivid clarity, the natural world in all its glory, feeling so much a part of it that the usual sense of duality dissolved. That phrase "pure perception," and its sister phrase "sacred outlook," had become the experience. Now, words fall away, useless.

Sacred outlook is what remains when the discursive mind quiets. The mind, wondrous instrument that it is, also colors, distorts, and manipulates our experience of reality in response to our lifelong conditioning. Spiritual practice, including training of the mind, slowly unravels that innate tendency.

It's one thing to have an experience of pure perception in the natural world but quite another to extend it to people and everything in the phenomenal world. The wise ones tell us that this is possible. That is the state in which they live, so the possibility is there for us as well.

I recently experienced how the force of pure perception could totally alter an extremely difficult interpersonal situation. In fact, what unfolded was so remarkable to me that I continue to marvel at whatever inner process invited it to happen.

For over five years I'd been working with someone whom I'll call Matt, whose expertise had helped me with projects I couldn't handle alone. We had become good friends, and I had come to rely on his help more than I realized. Matt had also been working for my partner Keith for a couple of years, but after several episodes that they saw from very differing perspectives, Matt resigned amid a lot of painful feelings. The fallout from this severance spilled over to Matt's relationship with me, and everyone's position, including mine, seemed intractable; Keith saw the situation one way, Matt saw it in another. I felt caught in the middle, distressed that I too was losing Matt.

Wanting desperately to find ways to mediate, I began doing a daily loving-kindness or *metta* practice for both of them, something I'd done in other contentious situations. One day, after a turgid and inconclusive conversation with Matt, it seemed clear that my mediating efforts were failing. Driven by frustration and helplessness, I totally lost it. I began to rage, ventilating to Keith as I explained that I wasn't mad at him or Matt, but at the situation. All my lofty intentions to mediate were shattered by the force of frustrated, raging feelings. I felt angry and helpless, totally locked into an intractable situation—of *their* making, I angrily thought to myself, bathed in my own righteousness.

Still feeling exasperated and deeply unsettled, later that same day, while walking alone in the beautiful spring afternoon, something shifted. I felt as though some mysterious force deep within had simply erased all the contentiousness, the opposing views, the whole entangled mess. I thought of these lines from a poem of Rumi.

Out beyond ideas of wrongdoing and rightdoing, there is a field.
I'll meet you there.
When the soul lies down in that grass,
the world is too full to talk about.
Ideas, language, and even the phrase "each other" doesn't make any sense.[11]

I was in that field. I could see Keith's point of view, and Matt's, and it didn't matter that they were different. I understood how each of them saw the situation and could honor them both without feeling any sense of conflict. Even my own tangle of feelings about the situation had been totally erased. I can only call it grace. I could also see that this was an experience of pure perception and marvel at what seemed like a small miracle.

This had been an astonishing experience. I continued to reflect on the idea of pure perception. One might think that it is simply a way of seeing or being in the world, but it is an active force, a view that affects those around the person who abides with that kind of open, accepting perception toward all. This is evident in spiritual teachers who reside in this state of unconditional acceptance and love under all circumstances. I'm reminded of His Holiness the Dalai Lama who holds no animosity toward the Chinese in spite of all the years of horror, torture, and violence that have befallen his people.

We're drawn to be around people like this. They awaken the highest within us, a kind of resonance, like a tuning fork that sounds a note that in turn awakens the same tone in another instrument. In the same way, they are tuning forks for us.

Most of us are unaware of how much our perceptions about people are filtered through the subtle lens of preconceived ideas, comparisons, and judgments. But there is another way to see—

through the lens of pure perception that assumes their basic goodness, even if it's hidden, as well as their capacity for kindness, unconditional love, and all the other positive qualities. I'm reminded of a simple yet humorous invitation that describes this perspective: "See people's light rather than their lampshade."

My experiences on the walk and with the interpersonal conflict both involved the mystery of grace. Words are inadequate for describing these experiences, but we can turn to the poets for help. William Blake comes to mind with his familiar words, "If the doors of perception were cleansed, everything would appear to man as it is, infinite."

He ends his long, illustrated poem with the words, "For everything that lives is Holy."[12]

Those inspiring words certainly apply to the compassionate activity of the woman in the next story. She saw every one of those humble sea creatures as worthy of being saved. How beautiful.

THE OLD WOMAN
AND THE STARFISH

T HIS STORY IS a wonderful reminder of how much each person matters.

※

An old woman is walking slowly along the edge of the sea. The previous night, a wild storm had hurled thousands of starfish up onto the sands, far beyond the high tide mark where they now lie helpless, soon to dry out and die. One by one, the old woman is picking them up and throwing them back into the sea.

A man approaches along the beach. He sees her vigorously throwing one starfish after another back into the ocean. Thinking that she must be crazy, he asks, "What are you doing? With all these thousands of starfish around, what do you hope to achieve? They're all going to die anyway. What possible difference can it make?"

The old woman picks up another starfish, glances at him with a glint in her piercing blue eyes, and hurling it with extra force, she answers, "To this one, it makes all the difference."

※

Like any compelling story, it continues to reverberate until we unravel its meaning for our own lives. Pierre Pradervand, in his beautiful book *The Gentle Art of Blessing*, uses this story to illustrate the importance of every positive thought we have, every kind word we speak, and every thoughtful action we take.

It also carries another message for me. Triggered by the haunting images of migrants, homeless and without a country, walking through southern Europe in search of a new home, I can't help but think about the tremendous suffering throughout our world, not only there but everywhere: the homeless, the displaced, refugees, drug addicts, criminals, the mentally ill—the endless list of all those struggling through seemingly hopeless lives.

They are the starfish. Everyone cast up on the shores of life, forgotten. Yet someone comes along and offers help, and something shifts. Through some small act, a life begins to turn around. Even the seemingly smallest act of kindness can make a difference. It reminds us that no matter how hopeless someone's situation seems, how broken and lost they appear, their essential self is always present. There is always a spark of humanity that can be reignited. People talk about wanting to make a difference, wanting to change the world. With the humblest acts of kindness or generosity, we change the world day by day.

I've always been intrigued by the mystery of how we touch one another's lives. It can happen through an action as in the previous story, or through words as in the next story, or simply through the force of a person's presence or any number of other ways. This gentle touching is happening all the time, and mostly we're unaware of it. It seems to be one of life's great secrets; we're constantly giving to one another in all these different forms and don't even give it a second thought. How wondrous! The last piece in this section describes how someone I never met gave me a radical new perspective on my life that I could never have imagined. He had written the message in four words on a chalkboard.

Memorable Messages

A S YOU ENTERED the meditation center, the library was the first door to the right. For a library, it was small. Rows of books lined the simply constructed, do-it-yourself shelving that covered three walls of the room. Flooded by the light of three tall, almost floor-to-ceiling windows, the room invited one to settle into one of the mismatched easy chairs that looked as though they'd been retrieved from a yard sale. The only sign of any system was a little sign that read, "Please return all borrowed books."

The selection covered fields like philosophy, psychology, and wisdom traditions. Primarily there were dharma books in the Buddhist tradition. After all, this was the Insight Meditation Society, one of the first retreat centers of its kind in the U.S., having just opened that summer of 1976.

I perused the shelves until one book caught my attention. Its pages consisted of a heavy stock held together by a plastic spiral. Clearly the book had been well-used as the pages were beginning to fall out of alignment. I pulled it out and looked at the title: *Sayings from the Chalkboard of Baba Hari Das.* The introduction explained that the author of these sayings was a *muni swami*, a term that meant he had taken a vow of silence. He'd already been silent for a number of years, and he communicated by means of a chalkboard.

At the time I was a householder with two young children: Ethan, nine, and Laura, six. As I read through the various exchanges Baba Hari Das had with his students, I came to one that stopped me in my tracks.

A woman asked, "How can I make any progress in my *sadhana* (spiritual practices) when I'm a householder with two small children?"

That was *my* question. I imagined the swami in the orange robes of a renunciant, leaning forward to write his answer on the chalkboard.

"Be a householder saint," he wrote on the board.

Only four words. I sat there in the overstuffed chair, sunlight flooding the page while the words reverberated in my awareness.

"How impossible," I thought. "He has no idea what it's like to have kids, intervene in fights, manage a household, and be in the midst of changing my field of work."

But the Swami's words wouldn't let me go. I ended up writing them on a note card, decorated the edges with a pleasing design, and placed it on my bureau where it stayed through several critical years—a gentle reminder, an impossible aspiration, and mysteriously comforting.

I never forgot the name Baba Hari Das. When I traveled to India several times for longer retreats, I wondered idly to myself where he might be, if he was still living, and whether he was still in silence, communicating by way of the chalkboard.

✿

Thirty-five years passed. That spring I signed up for a retreat at Mt. Madonna Center, located high in the mountains east of Watsonville, California, near the garlic capital of the world. Before leaving, someone told me that, by the way, the center had been set up—along with Mt. Madonna School—by an Indian swami name Baba Hari Das. How amazing! He was not only still living, but he was in California, not India. Maybe I'd have the chance to meet this mysterious swami whose four words had had such an impact on me.

Several days into the retreat, I learned that Baba Hari Das came to the Community Center for *darshan* (being in the presence of a spiritual teacher) several times a week so people could come and sit with him, report to him, ask questions, and simply be in his presence. It suddenly occurred to me that I could thank him for the memorable teaching I had received from him all those years earlier. By now, I'd told the story many times, shared it with parents, referred to it in talks, passed along this morsel of inspiration to others.

On the day of Baba Hari Das's next darshan, I set out down the hill from my room to the Community Center. As I walked along, I found myself having an inner dialogue with him. I began by thanking him for the householder saint message, and then I said inwardly, "*Now that I'm in the forest monk time of life, I wonder what his message might be for this stage?*"

Without any conscious thought, the answer arose immediately from within, "*Contemplate death. Be grateful and be joyful.*"

I entered the main hall where Baba Hari Das sat in a chair on a slightly raised dais. With his long white hair and beard, I imagined that he was in his eighties. He wore white robes, not the traditional orange of an Indian swami. There he sat, totally at ease, silent. Silent now, silent his entire adult life. Occasionally he looked around at two young children playing nearby and then toward the dog, his dog?

Everything was very informal and simple around him. No pomp and ceremony as with many such teachers. There was something both striking and ordinary about this scene; silence—his silence—was at the center, like a great well or primal source that radiated out all directions. Somehow the usual urgency of life seemed to dissolve, leaving me, and I assume most everyone else, with a sense of deep peace. All was well with oneself and the world.

Twenty or so people sat around, mostly silent, but sometimes talking among themselves. Someone would move forward close to his chair and say something, whereupon he leaned toward the little table at his side and reached for his writing board. The exchange went back and forth until it was complete. Then more silence.

After watching this protocol for about ten minutes, I moved forward to his chair. I told him about my first meditation retreat, how I found his book of sayings, how I discovered the perfect message for that stage of my life, how I'd copied it out, lived with it, and shared it widely over the years.

Then I briefly described the inner dialogue that I'd had with him just moments before as I'd walked down the hill to the hall. I repeated the message that had arisen for me. "*Contemplate death. Be grateful and be joyful.*"

Slowly he reached for his writing board, wrote for a moment and then handed me the board so I could read it. "*That is right.*"

Only three words. An affirmation of what I already knew to be the truth for this stage of life. I smiled, thanked him, and moved back to my seat.

PART III

❧

PASSAGES: DYING INTO LIFE

LIFE, LOVE, AND DEATH: INTRODUCTORY REFLECTIONS

W HEN I WAS in my thirties, a mysterious process started to awaken my deep and enduring interest in the subject of death and dying. I can now look back with the perspective of years and name the powerful influences that led to this awakening. These reflections entitled "Passages: Dying into Life" had their early roots from that time. Because this topic also relates to the theme of spiritual unfolding—whatever form that might take for you—I'll describe these influences, all threads that comprise this section. The story with which I'll begin towers above the others.

🙰

Twelve of us, along with three guides, are gathering for a weekend at a house deep in the country in northern Vermont. It's late summer and some of the trees are showing their fall colors, a melancholy harbinger of the hard winter to come. Many of us are therapists engaging in further training, although this time in a very unusual form. We've come to be with a medical doctor, psychiatrist, and well-known shaman from Mexico, a man whose reputation precedes him for his untraditional forms of therapy.

I am apprehensive about the weekend, because he's known to introduce his participants to very powerful shamanic journeys enhanced by the use of entheogens (meaning "God-enabling") like psilocybin or LSD, which often precipitate near death experiences, and cause powerful, out-of-body experiences. In his introductory lecture, he introduces us to shamanic traditions and sacred rituals, the borders between worlds, and the vast realities that exist beyond the confines of ordinary mind, as well as the deep healings that can occur not just personally but for others whose lives we touch.

He begins to lead us in various shamanistic practices, including drumming, sensory overload, and shamanic rituals, all of which lead to an accelerating tempo of utter chaos in sound and visual input. I feel as though I'm being assaulted from every direction—fast-moving images alternately beautiful, horrific, and violent that stream across three large screens—while wild drumming and then abrasive music simultaneously thunder through the room.

Ordinary consciousness can't sustain itself in the face of such an assault. I want to flee. Have I made a terrible mistake in coming here? Why did I consent to accompany Hob for this weekend, he—always the intrepid explorer of inner spaces, he—the incomparably fearless one. But something that feels like a deep calling of the soul keeps me here with my fellow travelers, for by now I feel we're all in this together.

At the climax of all this chaotic input, we're invited to put on eye masks that force us into intensifying, intrapsychic experience. Whatever the usual ways we hold on to our sense of identity, all that is being shaken, overwhelmed, and shattered by the rituals. I feel myself trying to hold on to some semblance of sanity, but various identities start slipping and gradually dissolving. The sense of "I" vanishes. Now just pure experience with no "I" to identify with any of it.

Wild images race across my inner visual fields—strange, frightening, and utterly foreign. A lot of rhythmic, ruthless beating of sound. I am dying. They are shooting me over and over and over again. I am in the Nazi war camps. I am everyman and everywoman who ever died by firing squad. I am standing against a glaring white wall, being mowed down by a stream of bullet-sound. I am everyone who has died in battle or shot in the street or killed in the jungle. I am dying over and over again.

The music is relentless, whipping consciousness from one extreme to another. Becoming a lion, roaring; becoming an African wildly dancing around a ceremonial fire with my black brothers and sisters; images of death, plane wrecks, death camps, piles of bones, all in whirling vortexes of color and sound, the intensity magnifying until something breaks open into another dimension. Somewhere in this timeless, spaceless stream of events, there is the faintest awareness of only wanting to find God.

There's no "I," yet now the vivid awareness of becoming a rocket, fire streaming out from the body, propelled from a launching pad and tearing upward into the cosmos. Fear beyond anything ever experienced. Sheer terror. A cataclysmic death exploding from deep within. Whatever fragmentary consciousness remains is catapulting through barriers, through confined spaces, through an endless tunnel at a million miles an hour.

Consciousness is breaking apart. Now dissolving. Then with one last effort, shouting, "I'm going! Oh my God. Take care of Ethan and Laura!" (Our children, then eleven and eight.) Dying. Streaming upwards into space, through the tunnel.

Then, the *breakthrough*.... All the moving images cease.... Into the light.... Clear Light, radiant Light. Light is everywhere, luminous, brilliant, gold, peaceful, blissful.... Timeless, spaceless, all One.... Beyond, gone beyond....

Gone beyond.... For how long? Timeless, spaceless, all One.... Light, always the Light....

Now the sound of sacred music.... Bach.... The B Minor Mass....

Consciousness slowly begins to reassemble, alternating between the pure Light and rainbow light. Alternating between the One and the multiplicity. The one Light and then the seven colors. Now a body of Light, now rainbow light.

A voice calls, a friend, I vaguely realize. "Olivia, where are you?"

"I'm in rainbows."

A fragment from a favorite Bach Cantata: "My soul there is a country afar beyond the stars, where stands a winged sentry...."

Knowing now this is the country of God. All of it: the music, Bach, sound, visions, vibrations, rainbows, light, pure being, and always the light.

Gradually vestiges of consciousness reassemble, ordinary reality like an old friend returning, except there is a profound difference. To the core of my being, I've experienced other realities, the "place" beyond time and space, beyond body and mind, beyond words that might describe it. There have been many deaths, especially dying to the little self, but what remains is level upon level of trust in the meaning of existence—an immense and awesome affirmation of this life and a life beyond. These insights are accompanied by extraordinary feelings of interconnectedness with everyone and everything, as though I've been woven into a vast web of loving connections. The heart's breaking open has been another powerful gift of this near death experience. Overcome with feelings of overwhelming love. Death, God, and love—the essence of this entire initiation.

The impact of this experience continued reverberating for weeks and months later. I wrote about it. I tried to paint the inner worlds I'd seen. I felt as though the primordial fear of death had been softened, though it would be hubris to claim freedom from that most universal of fears. Somehow the link between love and death had been insolubly forged. That was an extraordinary gift. In the face of death, love can always triumph—an inspiring promise.

"Life and death on one tether, running beautiful together." That was the poetic fragment that my husband Hob quoted, knowing that Alzheimer's would eventually take his life. Fourteen years my elder, he had had an insatiable curiosity about all dimensions of human experience including death. He taught the course on Death and Dying at our local university. We both started to do Hospice work and found ourselves accompanying loved ones who were dying.

Among those influences, there was also the deepening influence of meditation where deep states of absorption provided glimpses of going beyond the sense of "I." Beyond suffering—the promise of the Buddha's third noble truth—even beyond death.

I learned that in many Asian countries there are death-awareness practices, called *maranasati*, an ancient tradition considered by many to be the ultimate practice. As the Buddha said, "Of all meditations, that on death is supreme."[13] Although these may seem unusual or radical, opening to death as part of life feels entirely natural to me. Life becomes more precious. Just this precious, present moment. As one Buddhist teacher phrased it, "One learns the art of dying by learning the art of living: how to become master of the present moment."[14]

The following pages include an assortment of inspiring pieces that deal with loss, dying, and death. Dear reader, you may be asking yourself, *Why should I want to go there?* There are many answers, but perhaps the simplest one is that an awareness of death gives life vividness and immediacy. We realize how precious life is, the miracle of being alive, and how easy it is to take for granted.

Some of the most powerful parts of this section arose when Hob was slipping into the mists of Alzheimer's. "Bleached Bone," about grief, still evokes my tears these many years later. In the midst of such challenging, harrowing times, I seldom thought about the possible gifts of what we were going through. It felt more like an initiation by fire. But like the experience with the shaman, what ultimately shone forth was the deepening in love, the love that transcends even death. That is the central message of this section on "Passages."

DHUMAVATI: GODDESS OF AGING AND DEATH

S OME YEARS AGO, when Hob was already deep into the mists of Alzheimer's, I attended an exceptionally creative gathering of nine women, mostly in our fifties and sixties, who came together to celebrate a friend's fiftieth birthday. She had invited her friends—as their gift to her—to share some aspect of their expertise and wisdom, specifically to shed light on the challenges of aging.

One of the women, Diane, a healer from Santa Fe, had traveled across the country for the event. She was sitting on the floor across from me, wrapped in a woolen shawl woven in the rich, deep red colors of New Mexico's soil.

"All of us here are of a certain age," she began, "so perhaps it's time for us to be introduced to Grandmother Spirit, one of the wisdom goddesses from the tantric Hindu tradition. Her name is Dhumavati. It means 'smoke,' or 'the one who is composed of smoke.' Grandmother Spirit—I love that name. But you must understand that she's no benign figure sitting in a rocking chair! She's fierce and powerful, the one who wakes us up to the tough realities of aging just in case we've forgotten about that side of things."

Diane chuckled at the ripple of recognition from the rest of us.

"The tough realities of aging." My mind had already spun off into memories. That moment when the opthamologist became very silent as he examined my eyes through his scope and told me I had a deformity that caused glaucoma in my right eye and had already robbed me of more than half my vision. And later the macular degeneration—the tough reality that I might not make it through this life with my vi-

sion—the treatments, the injections, the operations. Tough realities. I already knew something about this aspect of Dhumavati.

As Diane continued, I pulled myself out of reverie. I had the feeling that Diane's teachings were striking each of us in a unique way and that a lot more was in the offing. I felt a familiar sense of unease in my gut; none of us wants to face the uncertain realities of aging.

"So, Dhumavati is one of the symbolic representations of the divine feminine in the Hindu pantheon. In her case, she symbolizes the sacred dimension of aging. So I think *we need her!*"

Diane's last statement was so emphatic, everyone broke into laughter. She rearranged her shawl and went on, describing Dhumavati as an ancestral guide who personifies the knowledge that comes from hard experience.

"She's no beautiful goddess. Not at all! She's a hag, like an elder form of Kali—fearful and ugly to behold—a reminder for us to look beyond outer appearances to find the deeper truths of life. Dhumavati's the one who introduces us to what is unknown, hidden, or feared in our lives, particularly as we age. So it follows that she also teaches us about the great mysteries of birth and death. She's even described as the wisdom of forgetting, an idea that's totally counterintuitive and maybe disturbing for those of us who are losing our car keys and forgetting our words!"

Again there was laughter. Again I spun off into images from my current situation.

"The wisdom of forgetting." How could wisdom and forgetting be linked? Hob is slipping through the veils into the confusion of Alzheimer's. He's sinking into the mists of mental loss, lost and adrift, sometimes anxious and fearful. Where's the wisdom in that? It's heartbreak all around. Sometimes when he speaks now, our two adult kids look at him in disbelief. What's happening to their father? Then one day he says to me, "This (Alzheimer's) is a different reality. It's not to be worried about." That blows me away. My mind stops, drops into total silence. Has he reached into some other dimension? An ultimate reality? Surely this is wisdom.

The laughter subsided. My attention came back to the group setting and some of the things Diane had said. I found something curiously comforting about a culture that acknowledged the unsettling realities of later life. This archetypal figure, with her strange ways, embodied the truths of aging in a bold, refreshing, and—yes—daunting way. Still I absorbed the images, grateful to receive another wise perspective at a critical time in my life.

Diane continued, "This wisdom goddess, forbidding and awesome as she is, forces us to seek for something deeper—the pure awareness that is beyond suffering. In fact, she shows us the gifts of suffering that we may discover after a really hard time. She takes us into unknown territory—into the void of forgetfulness, dullness, silence."

"Unknown territory." Suddenly I'm back with a terrible phase in my mother's illness, also Alzheimer's. She swings back and forth between raging with frustration and suffering silence. She's psychotic on top of the dementia, but the doctors haven't diagnosed that yet. No one knows how to help. She's driven so deep into her own psyche, she goes blind for two months. She cries out, "The people who are tortured, the people who are tortured," over and over again, plunged into some terrifying hell realm beyond our reach. My God, what unknown territory is she in? She's taking us all into unknown territory, and I feel utterly helpless to alleviate her suffering.

Diane's voice breaks into my tortured memories. I feel as though I'm hauling myself up from some dark, painful place to reconnect with what she's saying.

"But the nature of the void is pure consciousness. That's what we experience in meditation when the mind becomes still, totally absorbed, and we rest in our true nature.

"That's what Dhumavati is reminding us of—to move fearlessly into the unknown. She's not only about acceptance. She even honors that difficulty and sorrow are a natural part of life— something we know but keep forgetting. She teaches that with time and patience we'll discover that our hard times may lead to new insights, deeper wisdom, and more compassion toward ourselves and others.

I feel as though I'm ricocheting between realities, one of harsh and unrelenting suffering, the other inviting me to find the compassion in the midst of that suffering. I feel a flash of anger. How the hell are you supposed to do that? I can't bear to see my mother suffering. I can't bear that so many others are suffering with her, the demented, the wounded, the impoverished, the mentally ill, the dying. I know I'm globalizing, but where is the compassion in this? The paradoxes of life—terrible, unbearable extremes. Yet with a shift in view, these unbearable states are simply a part of life, and of death. I feel a subtle movement in my heart. Compassion is arising. Even in the midst of all this suffering, compassion is the only answer. And love.

Diane's voice brings me back. "One last thing about Dhumavati: she reveals that even sorrow and suffering have a sacred dimension, because they awaken in us the qualities we need to get through—perseverance, patience, courage, love. This Grandmother Spirit is one fierce and awesome figure! She embodies the wisdom teachings about later life. That's why I wanted to bring her here, because we all have something to learn from her."

A flurry of responses followed Diane's presentation—recognition of familiar issues, discomfort over the shadow side of aging, laughter over its inevitabilities. Strange as this unfamiliar imagery was, I felt as if Dhumavati had come roaring into this circle of women to wake us up, reminding us about loss and death in a culture that recoils from this natural process and fails to see our final passage as a highly significant time of life. On trips to India, I had seen their wide-ranging, exotic forms of worship. In the Indian village where I was staying, I witnessed how families took care of their dead, how they carried the body wrapped in white on litters, and accompanied by music, proceeded to the river where they handled the cremation themselves. No surprise then that India would have a goddess of aging and death to give meaning to life's greatest mystery.

The heart of tantric practice is to find the sacred in the ordinary, to find meaning in all aspects of life—even the most difficult. And to see everything in our lives as consciousness taking infinite forms. By introducing the dark side of aging, Dhumavati could help free us from attachments and reveal the deeper realities of later life.

How timely that Dhumavati came along—this strange figure with her compelling teachings. Symbolically, she veils everything so that we have to plunge beneath the surface to find hidden truths, to discover that we have the capacity for unimagined strength, to summon the courage to handle the crises. We can trust the love and compassion that will carry us through the seemingly impossible.

The Ultimate Mystery

A S WE LOOK into the great mystery that surrounds the sub-ject of death, we are humbled. We may have experienced the death of beloved family and friends, yet still the mystery stands before us. Much has been written; much has been spoken. Still we dwell in the realm of the great unknown.

Any book about aging must include this subject. As a way to address it, I have chosen the vignettes, stories, and poems that have most inspired me along the way. I find all of them heartening. They remind me of that simple phrase that my husband quoted as his world was slipping away through mental diminishment.

"Life and death upon one tether
And running beautiful together."[15]

Our culture has made life and death into antonyms whereas one could also say, perhaps more accurately, that *birth* and death are the true antonyms. The striking word in this poetic fragment is "beautiful." Death beautiful? How can that be? The poet is pointing to the obvious, that life and death are inextricably in-terwoven. You can't have one without the other. The presence of death reveals the preciousness of life. How ephemeral life is. In some of the sections that follow, the word "birth" is used in referring to death. Death itself is, of course, a finality, but the symbolic ways in which people write about it offer us wider per-spectives. Death is also birth into another dimension, into a new level of consciousness, into the mystery.

Here is a poem entitled "Dying is Becoming," one of four *Poems for My Mother* that my mother, Evelyn Perkins Ames, wrote in the months after her mother died. This poem is to my grandmother, introduced earlier in the book, the woman who looked at me with such unconditional love that I never forgot the moment.

Dying is becoming.
Only when she had gone was she completed
Or did we fully know her.
Dying is being born —
Though opposite of our propulsion from the womb,
Unseeing, unknowing, begun and helped by strangers:
This birth I prepare.
All my life I am working at it,
Not as before entirely blind
But multiplying, making, trying to sense the rightness
Of joining here, dividing there.
Meanwhile you do not know me, nor do I know myself,
Lacking the shadow that illustrates the round.[16]

The poem suggests that "this birth" that we call death is something we've been preparing for throughout our life, whether we realize it or not. Secondly, that the fulfillment of a life—its trajectory from birth to death—isn't known until death completes the circle of that life, "illustrates the round," as the last phrase says. The last chapter of a life is often particularly dramatic—how a person handles the final illness that comes to them, how they let go of the life they've led, how they surrender into their rapidly changing world.

I'd go even further than the poem's last phrase about completing the circle of a life. As I consider loved ones who have died, I recognize the subtle ways in which the relationship continues. It may be relationship only in memory, yet somehow the combination of time and one's own unfolding life provide a more complete perspective of the relationship. After my husband died, I came to see aspects of our relationship that had been hidden to me before. I noticed that the challenging parts of our relationship receded into the background, whereas the essence of our journey together shone forth with new intensity—that we'd been soul mates, supported each other's changing lives, and rejoiced in each other's independence. And that the love that originally brought us together was the deep river that continuously flowed beneath the surface ups and downs of our personalities.

For some people, however, even as death approaches, they still harbor unfinished business in their relationships; there are places that still need healing. If we cultivate the perspective that relationships are timeless and that subtle aspects continue after death, then the possibilities for healing are always there.

The truth is that relationships can be healed long after the other has died. This can happen through therapy or writing or inner dialogue with the deceased or a ritual or in the hidden recesses of the heart. I had a friend who had been in a difficult marriage, but after her husband died, their difficulties seemed to fade into the background and she gradually embraced more and more of what had been positive in their relationship. Was she living in denial? It didn't feel that way; it felt as though a new balance had emerged, that forgiveness and time had opened the way for greater acceptance and love.

Even with the finality of death, we continue to feel the force of the relationship, even to heal what was unfinished or broken. This is a hopeful realization, for all relationships have a timeless dimension.

What follows are perspectives on death from a writer, a philosopher, a theologian, a mystic, and a spiritual master, each with a unique message.

Death as Friend
Rainer Maria Rilke

In the days when written correspondence was the primary means of communication, one such prolific letter writer was Rainer Maria Rilke, the Bohemian-Austrian writer and poet who lived in the early twentieth century. On Epiphany in 1923, he wrote to a friend his reflections on the subject of death.

"Death is our friend precisely because it brings us into absolute and passionate presence with all that is here, that is natural, that is love.... Life always says Yes and No simultaneously. Death (I implore you to believe) is the true Yea-sayer. It stands before eternity and says only Yes."[17]

Rilke invites us to look more deeply into our ideas about these two words—life and death. We may have noticed that as we age we become able to hold the paradoxes of life with more acceptance and equanimity. For example, we may feel more passion for life because the presence of death is closer. Along with the inevitable losses, there are also the subtle gains. Even with a growing list of physical limitations, our love of life may increase. No one knows how much time remains, yet that contributes to life's greater intensity. Florida Scott-Maxwell, author of the classic book *The Measure of My Days*, stated that the decade of her eighties was the most passionate of all.

The world of paradox confronts us at every turn, yet we also sense another truth that embraces all the apparent disparities. Julian of Norwich spoke of this timeless truth: "All shall be well. And all manner of things shall be well."

THE INFINITY THAT IS YOU
Rabindranath Tagore

I find inspiration in the words of Tagore, the Indian visionary, philosopher, poet, and prolific writer who, in 1913, was the first non-European to win the Nobel Prize for Literature. Here is what he says about death:

"When I gaze at the infinity that is you, and lose myself in its beauty and vastness, Death and pain have no meaning, they are insignificant.

But when I turn away from you and center on myself, Death looms large and pain overwhelms me."[18]

As long as we can remember the larger perspective of infinity and lose ourselves in its beauty and vastness, then death and pain cannot overwhelm us, according to Tagore. This is an exalted perspective, yet Tagore's humanness is also embedded in these words.

SPIRIT OVER MATTER
Henry David Thoreau

With the natural losses that come with aging and illness, life-long attitudes toward the body are ruthlessly tested. Some people are fortunate to have cultivated such strength of mind—and perhaps spirit as well—that they handle physical challenges with greater ease. Thoreau, it seems, was one of these.

Thoreau's friend, Sophia Alcott, visited him in his last days and wrote this about her visit:

> "Henry was never affected, never reached by (his illness). I never before saw such a manifestation of the power of spirit over matter. Very often I have heard him tell his visitors that he enjoyed existence as well as ever. He remarked to me that there is as much comfort in perfect disease as in perfect health, the mind always conforming to the condition of the body. The thought of death, he said, could not begin to trouble him....
>
> One friend, as if by way of consolation, said to him, "Well, Mr. Thoreau, we must all go." Henry replied, "When I was a very little boy I learned that I must die, and I set that down, so of course I am not disappointed now. Death is as near to you as it is to me."[19]

THE GREATEST ACT OF LOVE
Henri Nouwen

I had the privilege of spending considerable time with Henri Nouwen, the Catholic theologian, priest, and author of forty books, many of them classics in religious writing. His time as a visiting professor at Harvard Divinity School had many challenges for him, not the least of which was the tension he experienced between Harvard's highly intellectual environment and his own longing for deep spiritual community. That longing eventually led him to leave his prestigious academic appointment to become the pastor for Daybreak, a L'Arche community in Canada that offers a welcoming, non-institutional setting for those with developmental disabilities. I often heard Henri say that these "special people" were closer to God than those of us who are without disabilities.

The most compelling course I ever took in all my years of academic study was Henri Nouwen's course on Spiritual Formation. The requirements were modest—radical in fact—for the Gospel of Luke was the only required reading for the semester! Granted, Henri handed out an extensive bibliography, but what we read was left entirely up to us. Among the other requirements, we were expected to attend Henri's lectures; we were to engage in *lectio divina* using one or two verses from the gospel as a springboard for writing a daily spiritual journal; and we were to find a spiritual director with whom we would share our journal for regular discussions. Whenever I revisit my journal from that course, my writing astonishes me. Something powerful and mysterious was at work throughout Henri's teaching and presence.

A charismatic speaker, Henri's passion for the life of the spirit was palpable and contagious. The large hall at Harvard Divinity School was always packed, including people who weren't even registered for the course. When Henri spoke, it seemed as though some invisible force streamed through him, igniting his words with passion. His intensity was so strong that some people in the room would spontaneously respond with sound or word as if in full resonance with the power of his words. I've seldom felt so spiritually nourished as I did in the space Henri created.

I offer this as background to provide context for what he wrote about death and dying, much of it gathered in a little book called *The Greatest Gift*. By this time his health was declining. Friends were dying, and the AIDS epidemic had exploded in our midst.

Henri's first response to his own struggles, which were lifelong and considerable, was to write a book. The following excerpts are from two of his books that deal with aging.

"Am I afraid to die?" Henri asks. "I am every time I let myself be seduced by the noisy voices of my world telling me that my 'little life' is all I have and advising me to cling to it with all my might. But when I let these voices move to the background of my life and listen to that small soft voice calling me the Beloved, I know that there is nothing to fear and that dying is the greatest act of love, the act that leads me into the eternal embrace of my God whose love is everlasting."[20]

"And so my death will indeed be a rebirth. Something new will come to be, something about which I cannot say or think much. It lies beyond my own chronology. It is something that will last and carry on from generation to generation. In this way I become a new parent, a parent of the future."[21]

Henri died suddenly of a heart attack when he was only sixty-four years old. Through his passionately lived life, his teaching, his books, and above all his presence, he left a remarkable legacy for all of us, whatever our philosophical orientation.

THE WORDS OF A MASTER
Master Sheng Yen

In the Buddhist tradition, the imminent death of a master teacher is considered a particularly powerful time, often the time for a final teaching. There are many stories, particularly in Zen, where the last words of the teacher are a final teaching treasure, often immortalized.

Such was the case with Master Sheng Yen, a revered Chan Buddhist Master who died in 2009 in Taiwan, his home country, at the age of seventy-nine. As an inspiration to Buddhists and non-Buddhists around the world, his last teaching was a poem he wrote just before he died.

"Busy with nothing, growing old.
Within emptiness, weeping, laughing.
Intrinsically, there is no 'I.'
Life and death, thus cast aside."[22]

What a beautiful example of the surrendered life—"busy with nothing, growing old." He embraces everything—the weeping and the laughing—and has gone beyond all sense of "I," an experience of freedom even beyond death. His simple yet profound words invite us to open to the liberating possibility that we too can experience this freedom.

These examples are exceptional and inspiring. You might be wondering how such exalted perspectives relate to our seemingly more ordinary experience. They provide us with a compass that orients us to the possible. We know there are no assurances about how our late life might unfold, but at some level, we can still prepare for living with the unknown—whether our own final years or days, or being with someone else at the end of their life. So it was with my friend Priscilla. We were definitely in the realm of the unknown, and our snatches of conversation revealed how we were trying to reach one another through the mysterious realms of consciousness.

BETWEEN REALMS

DONNA AND I are like sisters with our beloved friend Priscilla, and we know that her time is coming. Until illness stole away Priscilla's energy, the three of us had been meeting at dawn every week for over a year. Through every kind of weather including snow, ice, and sleet, we met in Priscilla's office, set up a simple altar, then chanted and meditated as a prelude to our discussions.

We were driven by the pain of spiritual disillusionment, examining what had gone awry in a tradition in which we'd practiced together. Passionate to uncover the truths, we plunged together into the abyss of betrayal, questioned the denials, named the abuses and the abusers—all in our quest for insight and healing. In the process, an unbreakable bond was forged between us.

❀

Now our beloved sister Priscilla is dying. As we come into her spacious room, a place of many gatherings during lighter times, we are surprised to find her not in bed as expected, but sitting in her mauve wingback chair by the window. The Hospice nurse, having just finished bathing and dressing her, has helped her across the room and into the chair.

Afternoon sun floods the corner of the room with light, illuminating the red, potted geraniums so they appear to be on fire. Next to the mauve chair, on a low table covered with deep blue Indian silk, sits one of Priscilla's altars. Always the artist, she must have created this altar when she was stronger, the Shiva statue draped with *rudraksha* beads sacred to Shiva, the unlit candle, the collection of natural objects—shells, stones—all carefully arranged.

Priscilla is very, very thin now, her face strikingly gaunt and pale, yet still, even medicated, her radiance shines through, though dimmed and more detached since our last visit.

"Oh, you've come. You've come. You've come to lift up my spirit," she says in a soft voice. As we hug, tears are streaming down her face, and mine, and she murmurs, "Yes, yes, yes. Yes, that's it. Yes."

I sense that we're in a different realm. We sit quietly. Priscilla, her eyes closed, seems to be on the edge of speaking. Her presence is curiously strong, yet at the same time very gentle, tender, tenuous, subtle.

"I don't know how to do this," she says in a soft voice, then pauses. "This dying. No one tells you how to do it." Another long pause, and then she continues.

"I have some things I want to tell you.... the people have been appearing.... they form a ring around me.... there are about ten of them.... they are my guides.... they are ordinary, dressed like you and me.... they're not in long robes or something, but like us.... their words are strong.... they're giving me knowledge and understanding and wisdom... protection... it's so peaceful there.... it's hard to come back..."

I can feel how hard she is concentrating to bring forth what she wants to say, as though she's drifting back and forth between states, reaching for words that will bridge the levels. I sense how much she wants to include us, to let us into this inner realm, these realms of consciousness she's now moving in. Somehow I know that this is her final teaching for us.

Out of the blue, with exceptional force, she says, "Writing helps.... it leads to the practices." But then the three of us have been writing a book together for well over a year, so the talk of writing is natural.

"Writing is a practice, as important as any practice.... the writing is a conduit.... like a straw.... like drinking divine water." She asks for water and speaks of her great thirst as she holds the water bottle.

"Writing is a channel.... it leads to things like Christmas trees and cedars." Perhaps she means that the spirit that inspires writing also manifests as trees and everything else? We start to fill in at various points, making intuitive leaps, amplifying her encoded words. "Yes, thank you. It helps when you help me.... the creative spirit is in art and music.... in everything.... there are a few things that still feel undone...."

I imagine she's referring to her parents with whom she has had an exceptionally afflicted relationship. They haven't come to see her even once during her illness. I mention that her parents are coming soon and that we should leave so she'll have enough energy for a difficult visit.

"They're coming?" she says, incredulous. "They're coming to see me? They're coming here? Really?" A dramatic moment, revealing what a big, unfinished piece this is.

"No, don't go yet. I don't even know what coming and going is any more... I want to change my dress for my parents' visit... help, I need help, but I don't want you to see my body."

"Pris, we are way beyond the body here. This is all about spirit now," one of us replies.

"Oh all right," she replies in a resigned voice. Her partner George and the Hospice nurses are the only ones she's allowed to see her body. We squeeze into the little bathroom and carefully, slowly help her to change into her favorite dress. There is a lot of banter about clothes, hair, and appearance, the three of us like teenagers getting ready for a party. From one reality to another, from the depths of her near-death soliloquy to this light-hearted banter.

Walking with slow, hesitant steps, we guide her back to her favorite chair. She carefully lowers her frail body into the chair. Her eyes are closed. We kneel beside her chair to say a few last words, appreciating our time together over the years, our deep bond, the healing we sought and found together.

"Priscilla, do you remember our reflecting bowl, our image of that imaginary bowl that graced the center of our little circle?"

"Of course," she murmurs, "our healing bowl."

We imagined that one of us would descend symbolically through the water of the reflecting bowl into the depths to do a piece of healing while the other two held us by deep listening and witnessing.

"Now, being with you, the image has shifted. Instead of one of us descending into the depths, I envision the energy of the reflecting bowl moving in an infinitely upward direction, carrying you upward toward the light, the boundless, radiant light."

"Ah, what a beautiful image," she murmured. A long silence. We each hug her in quiet goodbye and stand up to leave.

"I'll always be with you," Priscilla says in a very gentle voice, her last words to us, her two spiritual sisters.

THE FIVE REMEMBRANCES

IN A NUMBER of cultural traditions, there is some form of exhortation to remember our death. Some might recoil at this idea, dismiss it, call it morbid or depressing. Realistically, life and death are woven together in the wondrous tapestry of life—comings and goings, spring and fall, birth and death—all part of the natural order of things.

Maintaining an awareness of death is a wake-up call to the preciousness of life. People who receive a life-threatening diagnosis often comment how their priorities for living suddenly become dramatically clear. Several friends have told me that their illness was a gift. It transformed how they lived, their decisions, the quality of their days.

The Buddhist tradition has a practice called the Five Remembrances, phrases to contemplate as a reminder of life's ephemeral nature. Thich Nhat Hanh, the internationally known Zen master, has a particularly accessible translation of these ancient teachings:

> I am of the nature to grow old. There is no way to escape growing old.
> I am of the nature to have ill health. There is no way to escape ill health.
> I am of the nature to die. There is no way to escape death.
> All that is dear to me and everyone I love are of the nature to change. There is no way to escape being separated from them.
> My actions (karma) are my only true belongings, ... the ground upon which I stand.

The Buddhist teacher Pema Chödrön has shortened the remembrances to just three phrases: "Since death is certain, and the timing of death uncertain, what is the most important thing?" That last phrase is particularly provocative, especially in our culture freighted as we are with every conceivable form of distraction. We can ask ourselves that question when we turn for the thousandth time to our iPhone, email, or TV remote.

In other cultures, reminders about death are also often brief sayings, easy to remember:

In medieval times in Europe, there was an ancient practice of *momento mori*, remembering that I will die so I can live to the fullest.

The Native American expression is, "Today is a good day to die because all things are in order."

Carlos Casteneda, the illustrious Mexican shaman in the best-selling books of the 1960s, taught his students that death sits on our left shoulder, a reminder to wake up to the vividness of life and live like a warrior.

Finally, the Sufi saying, "Die before you die, and you won't die when you die." This saying refers to the ego and a reminder to commit oneself to whatever will transform it, for the more tenacious the ego, the harder it will be to let go into death.

In Zen monasteries worldwide, there is a wooden sounding block, the "han," that calls the practitioners to meditation. On it are inscribed the words,

"Listen everyone!
Great is the matter of life and death.
Awake, each one—
Don't waste time."

The Five Remembrances are a similar call to remember how precious life is. How easily we take our days for granted. How amazing it is, says the *Mahabharata*, an epic tale from India, that although we see death all around us, we don't expect it will ever happen to us. Yet a serious diagnosis or the loss of a loved one suddenly wakes us up to life's fragility. This core Buddhist teaching—the Remembrances—provides a realistic reminder of what's most important in today's rushing, distracted world.

Not surprisingly, conversations about death and dying don't occur that often until someone has recently died and the subject has been blown open by the dramatic circumstances. That's when we may hear stories about what people have experienced around the death of a loved one—altered states of consciousness, synchronicities, the appearance of ancestors, and so on. The stories often come with a rush of energy as though the telling itself breaks through ordinary realities and may be questioned by the listeners. Often these stories are reassuring and inspiring; they point to other realities every bit as "real" as what we call everyday reality. They intimate something we may unconsciously long for, beyond the reach of ordinary mind but resonant with some greater freedom that we know exists.

Many cultures accept the reality of these other realms, speak of them openly, and assume they are as much a part of the natural world as anything we experience with our ordinary senses. The following story is one that came down through my family, told with a bit of wonder because of the unlikely family member to whom it happened. Probably we've all heard variations on this story, because naturally many people experience unusual states of consciousness in the liminal phases between life and death.

THE THIN PLACE

A CCORDING TO TRADITIONAL Irish wisdom, there is a plane of consciousness between life and death that they call "the thin place." For some people, when they are approaching death, the reality of this dimension overlaps with the reality of whatever it is that follows death. We might also call it "the in-between place," where the dying person is still living in consensual reality but simultaneously opening to other dimensions of consciousness we usually can't imagine. This was our experience of being with Priscilla.

Many of us may have stories that illustrate the thin place, stories that are often passed around families because we find them strangely comforting and inspiring. When I was in my thirties Blanche, my other grandmother, died. She had been an outspoken, even virulent agnostic. I was wary about getting into philosophical discussions with her, certainly not about religion, because she was formidable, articulate, and clear in her views. In truth, I respected her more than I loved her.

※

GrandBee, as we grandchildren called her—the "Bee" for her name Blanche—was in the last couple of days of her life. One of her daughters, my Aunt Evie, was with her. GrandBee was in her bedroom in the large stone house that she and her husband had designed and built. The bedroom, with its heavy Victorian furniture, was spacious with tall, leaded windows looking upon the lawn and through the stately elms to the distant field where cows were grazing. She was sitting, slightly slumped, in the big, upholstered chair near the window, her eyes closed.

Out of a long silence, she began to talk quietly to no one in particular. My Aunt Evie was reading in the chair next to her and witnessed what happened next. There were silences between GrandBee's words.

"I'm seeing the light.... light up there.... in the corner.... of the ceiling.... my sisters.... my sisters are here.... now Mother.... and Father.... They are here.... talking without words.... they've come to get me.... my sisters.... come to help me across.... I see them.... they're here.... surrounded by light.... light everywhere...."

GrandBee fell silent as the vision faded. A day later, she died peacefully.

❊

This story about GrandBee's vision was passed around our extended family, a story that illustrates "the thin place" state of consciousness. Whatever GrandBee's opinions about mystical matters, when the moment of death approached, her vision of her family, particularly her sisters, appearing in the display of light was what unfolded for her at the end of her life.

Another story about the moments before death presents us with a different kind of mystery. In this case, the central figure was suffering from Alzheimer's disease. One of the greatest challenges of being close to someone with dementia is to decode the tangled ways in which they may try to communicate. You can feel their efforts to express some thought, but their ability to speak is hopelessly scrambled. At a certain stage of Alzheimer's or any form of dementia, the person may speak some nonsensical words, and then look perplexed or stunned. Eventually, they lapse into silence—sometimes for months or years. Not a word.

WHO SPOKE?

S OME STORIES HOLD us with their haunting power. The following one has reverberated in my memory for many years.
It turned my assumptions upside down and opened the doors of
possibility. The story is inspiring and hopeful. Having lived with
the intensity of Alzheimer's with the two people closest to me,
I am always affected by stories about dementia. My heart flies
open with feelings of connection and deep compassion.

Rachel Remen, M.D. is a nationally acclaimed medical re-
former and educator who regards the practice of medicine as a
spiritual path. A pioneer in recognizing the role of spirit in healing, she is the Founding Director of The Remen Institute for the
Study of Health and Illness (RISHI) at Wright State University, Boonshoft School of Medicine, Dayton, Ohio, Professor of
Family Medicine at Boonshoft School of Medicine, and Clinical
Professor of Family Medicine, UCSF School of Medicine, San
Francisco, CA. She heard this story at a medical conference as
recounted in her best-selling book *Kitchen Table Wisdom: Stories
That Heal*.

THE QUESTION

For the last ten years of his life, Tim's father had Alzheimer's
disease. Despite the devoted care of Tim's mother, he had slowly deteriorated until he had become a sort of walking vegetable.
He was unable to speak and was fed, clothed, and cared for as
if he were a very young child. As Tim and his brother grew
older, they would stay with their father for brief periods of time
while their mother took care of the needs of the household.

One Sunday, while she was out doing the shopping, the boys, then fifteen and seventeen, watched football as their father sat nearby in a chair. Suddenly, he slumped forward and fell to the floor. Both sons realized immediately that something was terribly wrong. His color was gray and his breath uneven and rasping. Frightened, Tim's older brother told him to call 911. Before he could respond, a voice he had not heard in ten years, a voice he could barely remember, interrupted. "Don't call 911, son. Tell your mother that I love her. Tell her that I am all right." And Tim's father died.

Tim, a cardiologist, looked around the room at the group of doctors mesmerized by this story. "Because he died unexpectedly at home, the law required that we have an autopsy," he told us quietly. "My father's brain was almost entirely destroyed by this disease. For many years, I have asked myself, 'Who spoke?' I have never found even the slightest help from any medical textbook. I am no closer to knowing this now than I was then, but carrying this question with me reminds me of something important, something I do not want to forget. Much of life can never be explained but only witnessed."

⚜

Who spoke? I too have pondered this question. In fact, this story has touched me deeply, so much that I've come to feel an inexplicable connection to Tim and his father. Having given many talks to various groups, including hospices, Alzheimer's groups, medical settings and so forth, I almost always tell this story. Why has it touched me so deeply? Because I sense that the story has a hidden gift; it invites us into the place of mystery. It's my intuition that even if the brain is largely destroyed, there remains some fragment of consciousness that knows, that hears, that exists on some level beyond our ideas about consensual reality, that is the essence of the person, ravaged brain or not, that may even speak with a last message like Tim's father.

Tim, the cardiologist, explains that many things in life can only be witnessed and must remain inexplicable. I've heard of several other instances where a loved one has spoken out of the blue after months or years of silence, usually toward the end of life or very close to death, with one last message, even if only a few words. These moments are referred to as "terminal lucidity," a cool, clinical phrase for something that may lie much deeper in meaning than medical efforts to name it. In talking about subtle states, words become problematic; they limit, restrict, and reduce the ineffable, the mysterious. Sadly, they may invite reactivity instead of possibility.

That there is consciousness beyond the mind provides a place of wonder, of promise. Even if our loved one is totally unresponsive, without affect, with the frozen expression of the seriously demented, we can still remain open to the possibility of there being some deeper level at which they can be reached. This is the impact of Tim's story and others like it. It doesn't matter that we can't know for sure. We can accept the premise that consciousness is present. The invitation is to treat the demented person with love and respect, to speak to them as one always has, as if they were fully present, and most important, to trust that some part of them, however infinitesimal, will be touched by our compassion.

THE GIFT OF DEATH

My mother's name was Evelyn. She was known affectionately as Evvie. She was a writer and poet, someone who loved words, who was highly articulate, and loved nothing more than a lively conversation. In her mid-seventies, her words began to slip. Her actions became hesitant. Her walk slowed to little halting steps. She would look confused, troubled. At that time, the operative phrase for her advancing condition was senile dementia, something both her parents had suffered from. The word Alzheimer's, a specific form of dementia, was just beginning to appear. No matter what one called the process, all of us, including her, were in various stages of disbelief and denial.

The disease continued to work its ravages. Finally, she ended up in a nursing home where she lived for six years. For over a year and a half, she hadn't spoken at all. Occasionally she made a heart-rending noise like a wail that I could only interpret as her immense frustration at not being able to communicate. Her gift of words had now long gone.

In the last couple of months of her life, she lapsed into a coma. She appeared to be sleeping, her eyes slightly open but glazed. One day toward the end of January, she had a bout of high fever and the nursing home staff thought she might be dying. The night of her high temperature, I was in India. As she was burning with fever halfway around the world, I had an unusually restless night with one dream after another about my mother. I felt uneasy about being so far away, but I had to wait three more days until my flight home.

Meanwhile, my sister Joanie flew from Cambridge, Massachusetts, to Long Island to be with Evvie. That's when the first striking episode occurred. Joanie had been there for a couple of days, the fever had subsided, and Evvie seemed to have stabilized. In a moment of despair, uncertain about whether to stay or leave to return home, Joanie laid her forehead on Evvie's shoulder and said, "Ma, I don't know what to do." To Joanie's amazement, Evvie, who had made no sound for many months, started vocalizing. She was making talking sounds in her throat with her mouth shut. Joanie was startled by what was clearly Evvie's effort to communicate. Not only did Joanie decide to stay, but she called me to come right away—by now I'd returned from India—and Joanie spent that night sleeping on the floor in our mother's room.

The next afternoon, three of us—my sister and I and Marge, my mother's favorite companion—were gathered around her bed. Evvie was in a coma—and it's well known that people in comas can hear—and Joanie declared, "Ma, this is very special; you have both your daughters here together now!"

As often happens when people are close to death, they wait until certain loved ones come. We sensed that perhaps this was what she had been waiting for—for my return from India and for both of her daughters to be there with her. By now we all sensed that death was near. We'd spent the afternoon reading her poetry to her, playing the Mozart Requiem, and sitting quietly with her. I did several rounds of the clear light meditation for the dying, an approach in which I had trained.

With a storm raging outside, afternoon moved into evening. Evvie's irregular breathing continued, a phase the nurses said might continue for a while. As Marge stood by, Joanie and I, both thoroughly conflicted, began to discuss what to do about dinner. Our father was expecting us to come home for dinner, and we'd already called him twice to delay the time. As we stood by her bed trying to make a final decision, Evvie literally started to move in the bed. It looked almost as though she was swimming. At the same time, she started vocalizing again, the same guttural effort to speak, although now it was even more forceful and prolonged than the previous time. She continued to move and make her sounds until I sat down on the bed, put my hand on her shoulder, and said quietly, "Ma, we're not going anywhere. We're staying with you."

At those words, she stopped moving and became silent. Flat as her expression had been for months, when she heard those words, her face seemed to relax into a very subtle smile of contentment. All three of us recognized what had just happened; she had heard and understood our conversation. On some level she was fully aware; even though she was now in the dying process, she had gathered enough remaining energy to let us know—clearly—what she wanted.

Then she began to make humming sounds on her out-breaths, a lovely, almost contented sound. She seemed completely absorbed in this last act of living. As I covered her hand with mine, Joanie stood by her head, Marge by her feet. I resumed the clear light guiding with its suggestions for letting go into the light that is visualized at the time of death. The three of us sat, totally attentive, fully absorbed, breathing and humming very quietly in rhythm with Evvie's breaths—a loving, sharing chorus, her breaths as delicate as butterfly wings. The pauses between her breaths became longer. In one of those spaces, I had the flickering image of a child learning to swim off a dock, swimming away, then coming back, each time venturing further out, experimenting with being free then returning to the known, in this case, the body she was in the process of leaving.

Then another breath, a longer pause, the trace of a breath, and then the breath was gone. She was free. Joanie leaned forward and whispered into a great void, "Ma, you've done it!"

There lay our mother's lifeless body, yet up came our joy and rejoicing. She was finally freed from the sufferings that had ravaged her body and mind. With the Mozart Requiem playing once again, we shared tears and hugging. Surprisingly, mostly we shared feelings of celebration. After such prolonged suffering, Evvie had died peacefully, a beautiful death, her final gift. The grief would come later. Now the room seemed to fill with energy, subtle and strong, as if her presence now radiated everywhere. She was free at last.

This story illustrates once again the mystery around those whose minds have been destroyed by dementia. Through some means, often supremely subtle, they may reveal that some fragment of their consciousness is still there. They are hearing. They are taking in our words. They may give us a sign that they understand. My mother clearly communicated to Joanie without words. Again, in the last hour before her death, and even more dramatically, she gave the three of us a clear message, and we all got it.

May we always remember: no matter how devastated the demented brain may be, there is still some trace of consciousness beyond the mind that we can touch with love.

The grief came later. Like death itself, grief is a mysterious, unpredictable process. It comes in cycles. It strikes at the most unexpected moments, triggered by a piece of music, memory, dream, anniversary, or anything that echoes from your past with the one who has died.

BLEACHED BONE

WALKING UP THE hill in a bitterly cold, damp fog, the wind bites through my jacket. A November day in Vermont, dark with overcast, sullen harbinger of winter. Today is a year to the day since he died. Someone told me that twenty-two—the number of his death day—is a master number. He was born on the twenty-second as well. What symmetry. That momentary uplifting thought is soon obliterated by emptiness. I continue climbing the hill toward our meeting place, writers gathered with a shaman for his writing workshop. I'm not sure how to be present when I'm knotted with resistance, disconnection, unexpressed grief.

The moment I enter the meeting room, I see it, my eyes magnetized to that one object among many, a round piece of bone with wings and spire, the vertebra of some large animal. It rests like an all-seeing eye on the mantle above the blackened fireplace. Bleached with time, brilliant white, almost glowing, the gothic eye of bone stares out into the room. The bone sees a woman standing silently, looking back at it. Her breast plate is etched in bone-white grief, signature of loss, a year since that last breath, when, with a moan like woman's labor, he left, the soul freed to soar.

Back then—and now—time compressed into one vivid moment, she sits alone in silent reverie, visualizing the light into which he has gone, the body empty, a chrysalis out of which new life has been born. She remembers the washing, the anointing, wrestling the inert form into his ordination jacket, transforming the room into sacred space for all to come for last farewells. She goes through the rituals as if moving underwater, handles everything in a dreamlike haze. She's living a half-life now, her breath dry and shallow like a sun-blasted creek bed, shriveled, cracked, crying out for rain.

She wants to retreat to a dark cave lined with lichen and moss where the Earth Mother dwells, the One who waits upon the grieving. The Mother is dressed in softly falling skirts of deep red and purple. Her tunic, woven of earth colors, is adorned with brightly colored beads. Her long, dark hair falls around the younger woman's head as She gathers the exhausted form into arms made strong by tending the animals and growing things that sustain Her vast extended family. Her breath, deep and rhythmic, warms and caresses the bereaved woman's weary body.

How long the journey had been with her beloved, the journey that led into forgetting, confusion, dissolution, and death. The younger one had stood by, holding an inexorable process, her life woven into complex patterns of helplessness and hope, rage and despair, grief and love.

The soft, strong body of the Earth Mother holds her through the timeless dark while hot, bounteous tears water the floor of the cave. She had needed to be a warrior for so long, her grief had, by necessity, been stifled. Now in the arms of the Mother, grief erupts, finally let loose in heaving waves of tears.

"Beloved one, where are you?" the younger woman cries out. "You, the sound of Bach suites, talking blues, flamenco guitar. You, the lover of words and poetry. You, the bringer of laughter and delight. You, the wounded one whose heart finally blossomed like a wild lotus. You, in that final dream, the saffron-colored fish swimming in graceful elegance in a pristine mountain pool. You, the flock of multicolored birds wheeling above the precipitous cliffs. You, my soul friend who has gone, gone, gone beyond."

She falls silent. Still the Great Mother holds the woman as she weeps, tears swelling into rivulets that course through the emerald green moss. The Earth Mother's compassion has allowed the grief to spend its force, has embraced every raw and anguished feeling that has racked the younger woman's body. To everything there is a season, an end—even deep grief.

New life begins to stir around the two figures, improbable green thrusting up through the loam of last fall's leaves, browned, rotten, yet rich with life. Tiny arbutus plants open their white petals, crescent moons in clusters, releasing their sublime fragrance, blessing the Earth Mother and her child.

The grieving woman now knows her place of refuge, a hidden cave where dwells the Earth Mother, the one who can hold all things. Through Her, the grief will be healed.

A GIFT OF LIFE AND DEATH

Excerpt (Anonymous)

I want my death to be a gift, a birth.
When in that final breath
I breathe myself back into God
I want to be drawn into you also,
into the world of stars and earth,
plants and birds and animals,
into the roaring sea.
I want to be an intimate part
of all the universe.
And so, as I am breathed back
into the heart of this world,
into the hopes and dreams
and joys of the people,
into the yearnings
and the tears and the sorrows of this world,
my death will be a birth, and a gift.

PART IV

�֍

WAYSHOWERS

WAYSHOWERS:
INTRODUCTORY REFLECTIONS

I DON'T REMEMBER when I first heard the word "wayshower," but in the same way that children learn new words, it crept into my vocabulary without my noticing. From the start, I loved the word. We find our "way" through life in a similar manner to the Quaker expression "as the way opens," and all along we have those who show us the way—parents, teachers, friends, authors, mentors, spiritual teachers, guides of all kinds.

Because of the centrality of spirituality in my life, when I first started thinking about wayshowers and how to write about them, I assumed they would be mostly wise teachers, eminent in their traditions, masters of meditation. Upon deeper reflection though, that proved not to be the case. It turns out that this is a more multi-faceted subject than I'd originally thought.

As I thought about it further, I realized that my spiritual teachers had, of course, been wayshowers, but in a much wider context, one that went beyond any single issue such as aging. They were simply far larger than any one category. Their presence was timeless. In a way, they all belong in this section, but that would make it too crowded!

Although many others embody qualities that inspire me, I've chosen six people to present here as my primary wayshowers. The process of choosing surprised me as much as anyone. Each one beckoned to me, asking to be included because of something unique about how they'd lived their lives and the perspectives that inspired them. These wayshowers include two artists, two beloved friends, an eminent spiritual teacher, and an elder with whom I had only the briefest encounter. The last person would be astonished to find herself in such company; yet such is the mystery of how we touch each other's lives.

Dear reader, my thoughts turn to you. Who might your way-showers be? Perhaps you haven't thought about it in this particular way, or you use other terms like mentor, guide, or teacher. But I love the word *wayshower* for its particular relevance to the subject of aging. They are the ones who've gone before us, who have modeled ways of being that touch us deeply, and who embodied wisdom in the way they lived the most challenging chapter of their life. I bow to each and every one of them.

Photo courtesty of Dinah Starr

POLLY THAYER STARR

FOR ALL SHALL BE WELL
POLLY THAYER STARR

POLLY WAS NINETY-SIX years old when we first met. How surprising when a deep friendship blossoms suddenly, especially at a time in life when circles of friendship are already well established and things are ordinarily winding down. But little was ordinary about my relationship with Polly.

My father and stepmother, residents of the same elder community, invited Polly to join us for dinner. They told me about her, what a gifted artist she was, how she still had a one-woman show at a major Boston gallery almost every year, that her paintings hung in the Museum of Fine Arts and other leading museums. What a lively person she was, they said, in spite of being both blind and hard of hearing, infirmities she handled with remarkable ease.

We settled into a quiet corner of the dining room, and Polly and I exchanged the pleasantries of a first conversation. After hearing the briefest reference to my interests in psychology and meditation, she leaned closer and said quietly, "It's hard to believe, but in a place like this no one is interested in talking about death—what writers say about it, the mystery of it, anything. I've tried here and there, but people shut down or change the subject. How can they be at the end of their lives and not be interested? It's extraordinary, really."

That's how our friendship began. And once she heard that I shared her interest and had worked with Hospice, she kept inviting me back for lively conversations over tea. It became a ritual.

We'd plunge into talk about finding meaning in life, aging, death, and dying. She relished exploring the unknown. I marveled at her energy, her intense curiosity, her hunger for depth, even passion as we talked about the mysteries of life.

Polly has just celebrated her hundredth birthday, and once again I find myself walking down the long hallway that leads to her room. I knock loudly and hear her familiar call, "Come in." I feel my own anticipation as I enter her living room and see her, as always, sitting on the blue couch with her somnambulant cat, Benny, curled up in her lap.

"I'm so glad you've come," she says. "We must pick up where we left off. What did you call it? Oh yes, life review." It's so like her to plunge right in as she invites me to pour the tea. Because of her blindness, her eyes are slightly closed, her face framed by a crown of white curls. I'm always aware of her deafness, not only because our conversations are woven with repetitions or her requests that I speak louder, but because I too am hearing-impaired. Her struggle to hear probably accounts for the characteristic tilt of her head, alert to the subtlest nuances of my voice. Her alertness is striking, as though every sense is heightened, every moment electric with possibility.

"I've been thinking about faith," she begins, " how the form that my faith took in my forties isn't satisfying my needs today. I need a whole new going over as far as faith is concerned. We keep changing in our lives right up till the end. The difference between eighty and one-hundred is enormous!

"I've had a realization with time, thought, and prayer," she continues, "that faith works subconsciously at night. It's working inside. And I believe all the other lacks in me will be filled before I die."

She stops speaking, as if taking in the implications of what she has just said. Her face is animated, her voice strong, and her mind totally engaged in this invitation to review her life. Her recollections are coming in pieces, like bright colored pieces of glass in a stained-glass window. Now she starts talking about being a mother.

"Just when I think I'm getting somewhere with understanding that phase of life, I realize maybe I was wrong, that I made mistakes that I didn't see then. I rejoice that I didn't make all the mistakes I might have made! I'm doing a reassessment now. I need to work on me!"

She pauses and starts stroking Benny with slow, loving hands. Her hands are thin, mottled with brown, her veins prominent. Benny starts to purr gently while she continues, "Dede, my helper, has been rereading letters from my family and friends. It's wonderful to hear them. I can now see my life with them—and through them, through their eyes. I had no way of doing this before. At that time, I didn't pay attention to what they were saying, but now I have a whole new context for understanding my life, our friendships, how we touched each another.

"Oh, time is too short! What we're talking about—this life review—it makes me want to keep going!"

We chuckle together. And then, as if in anticipation of what she's about to say, she sits up a little straighter. Benny stirs in her lap. "Back to this subject of faith. I want to tell you about something that really deepened my faith. It happened a long time ago, when I was twenty-eight and in art school in France. One afternoon, I went riding in Fontainebleau forest, a wonderful experience—the beauty of the forest, riding along with the light coming through the trees.

"I came home and lay down on my bed, still in my riding clothes, when I slipped into a totally indescribable state of consciousness. I don't know what happened. All I know is that for an hour or two—so that I missed dinner—I lay there experiencing what William James calls a peak experience. I was in an atmosphere of heaven—an entirely different universe. I knew that everything was all right about my life, about everyone and everything. I even knew that everything was all right from the past and forever forward into the future.

"I had a whisper of the same experience again just before I had a miscarriage and lost a child. I had this same feeling that everything is all right, and that we're looked after. Words just can't describe it, but the experience has stayed with me for my entire life. I feel absolutely safe.

"Peak experiences are timeless gifts. Which reminds me of that quote, the words God spoke to Julian of Norwich, the fourteenth-century mystic, during a near-death experience she had when she was in her thirties: 'For all shall be well. And all shall be well and all manner of things shall be well.'"

Polly pauses, then continues. "Those words are all about faith, a kind of ultimate faith."

I hesitate to interrupt her ruminations. But she's silent, so I speak. "What a remarkable experience, Polly, your state of consciousness that afternoon. A lifelong gift for you, but also for us with whom you share that story. Thank you."

Polly and I have several other conversations over the next few months where she continues to reminisce about her life, her marriage, her father's suicide, her self-judgments even about her art. Despite her extraordinary gifts as an artist, she still feels she could have done more. We laugh together over internalized familial pressures to achieve—that no matter what we do, we could always do more, or better. Even at age one-hundred, this pesky self-judgment persists. She can hardly believe it herself.

Polly had turned 101 when I had come for one of my last visits. Again she is sitting on the couch, this time with Benny stretched out along the back near her shoulder. Her eyes are closed.

Words don't seem to matter in the same way anymore. From her vivid, inquiring, intensely-engaged self, Polly seems to have shifted into another rhythm, perhaps another dimension. Our conversation takes on a less urgent, gentler tone. We're simply sharing each other's presence, exchanging occasional bits of conversation, alternating with easy silences.

Several times, she seems to slip into what seems like a suspended state, as if she is disconnecting from ordinary reality and experiencing another level. Her expression becomes static, as if temporarily frozen from the moment her consciousness shifts. Her eyes are mostly closed, her mouth slightly open, her face immobile.

I remain quiet. Waiting. After several minutes, she speaks. "I'm experiencing in-between moments," she says quietly. "I feel as if I'm somewhere else. It feels spacious, complete, completely one. I can let go and let go. It's a wonderful feeling. Very safe."

When I ask if she can describe this state any further, she replies, "There is no feel to it. It is simply everything. Completely one." Long pause, and then she continues. "When I was at Quaker meeting, I often used to wonder how to be with that silence. I needed something to hold onto in the silence. It was too formless for me."

I remind her of a simple way to focus the mind that we've talked about before, by repeating "clear mind, peaceful heart" with the in-breath and the out-breath. She brightens with the recognition.

"Oh yes, I remember. I tried that. It helped. Can we do it again?" Again she drifts away, seemingly suspended in a state of consciousness beyond this moment, this place. Whatever is happening for her, it seems effortless, moving in and out of levels of consciousness in a way that has its own momentum. Perhaps this is a gentle preparation for death, an association I'm making from watching my own mother in her own last days.

When Polly stirs slightly and asks, "Can we do it again?" I begin to repeat the phrases quietly, coordinating with her breath.

"Clear mind... peaceful heart. Clear mind... peaceful heart."

The phrases come further apart. I sense now that she may have fallen asleep. After a while, I get up and start to leave. I look at her once more. Maybe she's sleeping, maybe she's somewhere else. Benny hasn't moved. The room feels filled with silence and stillness. The words arise spontaneously, "All shall be well. And all shall be well and all manner of things shall be well."

Photo courtesy of Ron Goodman

EMERSON STAMPS

BROUGHT HERE TO LOVE
EMERSON STAMPS

"**M**Y FATHER WAS conceived in slavery, but he was born free," says Emerson to our meditation group. He makes this astonishing statement in a matter-of-fact voice.

There's silence while we try to take it in, everyone undoubtedly thinking whether this is possible. I'm wrestling with the math. It's May 2010. The Civil War ended in 1865, 147 years ago!

"Your *father!*" exclaims Richard out of the silence.

"Yes, my father was born in 1865 right after the Emancipation Proclamation, and he was sixty when I was born. And I'm eighty-seven. That makes 147 years. That's how it works."

Our discussions arise from the half-hour meditations that start our meetings. There is no agenda, no leader, just the unfolding of whatever interests are circling around spiritual issues or the concerns of one of our members.

In his mid-eighties, Emerson decided to write about the highlights of his life, a powerful book entitled *Don't Look Them in the Eye: Love, Life, and Jim Crow.*[23] He was born on a farm in Arkansas, the land having been given to his family under the forty acres and a mule provision that followed the Civil War. As he started to write, "it was like a tape playing in my head," he said to me. Then he began describing a prenatal memory. "On the night I was to be born, there was a gathering of people, souls around.... They came to me, angels or whoever they were, and said, 'There is a family that needs love and we know you can handle this. We're going up to the gate (that leads into life) and you can leave. You'll be supported all the way through. You'll be supported by us.'"

As his life story unfolds, Emerson seemed to have been chosen for a daunting task yet was supported and protected in the most extraordinary ways. The first sentence of the book says, simply, "My first memory was the cotton sacks." Like the other mothers, his mother used to place him on a cotton sack and drag it along behind her through the fields as she picked cotton in the stifling heat of the day. When he was about two years old, Emerson couldn't bear to see his mother laboring in the fields, wringing wet with sweat, the backbreaking work relentlessly driven by the landowner.

"I was figuring out how to save my mother from the fields before it killed her. I consciously made myself sick, ran a fever, so she'd have to stay home with me."

As a child, he had the exceptional gift of being able to move between realities, what he calls the cross-over. "I think we all live in parallel universes. I think when you're a kid, you can see and be a part of both universes. I think that was what was happening to me. When I was little, and I was on that cotton sack, and saw my mother's suffering, I couldn't tolerate that. I just went where I thought was never-never land. I didn't see anything any more, and I kept going back and forth until I was told in this other place that I couldn't come back any more, because I was getting too old to do this. I had to stay in the other reality. That was very vivid to me, and I remember every bit of it."

Although Emerson doesn't dwell on the hardships of his childhood, he does describe some of the violence, anger, and turmoil in his family, how as a toddler he went around hugging everyone, trying to bring some love into his dysfunctional household in spite of being rejected and chastised for his hugging. Confused and frightened, he stood there, abandoned and trembling, unable to understand all the violence that made his family like "a living hell."

Some years later as a curious child of nine, Emerson was watching a storekeeper at work, forgetting his father's teaching that you never look a white person in the eye. The shopkeeper turned on him. "Boy, I don't want you in the store. A cross-eyed nigger and a black cat is bad luck," and he was thrown out of the store. He fled to his brother's truck and wept.

In one episode after another, Emerson seemed to survive the impossible. There was the time his brother was speeding and misjudged passing another car. In a devastating head on collision that left the car a mangled wreck, Emerson, still holding on to his little daughter, was thrown free of the car. He felt as though he was "flying in a bag of air." He never felt a hard landing or sliding along the pavement. His two-month old son landed unhurt in the grass. Although his daughter had a broken leg, Emerson didn't have a scratch on him. His brother and the others were killed.

Emerson also describes his time during the Second World War when he was in the first line of ships in the D-Day invasion of the Normandy beaches. Bombs were falling all around his landing craft, but his ship was never hit. In the middle of an electrical storm that broke over them during the landing, he was hit by lightning that came down a wire and grounded at the winch he was holding. He could see fire all around him but felt no heat, nor the current coming through him "It was as though I wasn't there." No one could understand how he survived.

Later, on the fields of Normandy, he escaped the strafing of German bombers and one crisis after another where he could have been killed. Amazingly, amid the chaos and death of the D-Day invasion and the weeks that followed, he never felt that anything was going to happen to him. He trusted his mother's letters telling him "I'm praying for you." He was never afraid, he said, because he "knew" the combination of prayer and his life's purpose would protect him.

After the war, his career took him into psychiatric social work, an advanced degree in psychology, and a lifetime of serving others, whether his patients, church community, strangers, or his family. A high point came early in his career when he assumed leadership in unionizing mental health workers for the first time in Kansas. Propelled to action, even calling for strikes that temporarily closed the hospital, Emerson was quoted in *Time* magazine in 1968 in an article entitled "The Revolt of the Aides."

Most striking, however, and running through his life from infancy to his late eighties, was a rare sense of his life's purpose: he was brought here to love. By nature a modest person, he doesn't talk about his inner life unless he's invited to speak about it. He lives easily with the unseen worlds and with his gifts of knowing.

Hob considered Emerson one of his two spiritual brothers, and in the months following Hob's death, Emerson would tell me in the most matter-of-fact way, "I talk to Hobbs almost every day," as if it were the most ordinary occurrence. Now in our group, we're talking about our families and how we sense the presence of family members who have died.

"So, Emerson, how do you feel the connection with people who've died?" I ask him.

"It's no big deal. I just change stations," he replies. "I still live in my family that includes all those who have passed over. I feel that my deceased sisters and brothers are still here. About life, we're supposed to dance, enjoy, and celebrate. I grew up going to a church where they were always connected to the spiritual side, the benefits of prayer, where the pastor was really into spirit and used a lot of vivid images. I loved that part of church.

"I don't feel old in my thinking. As long as I'm healthy, I can be useful. I asked the universe how long I'd live. Just like that, the answer came: ninety-six. It's not dying, but passing from this existence into another. To think about transferring out; that's easy. That doesn't bother me. It's going home. Life here is just a temporary existence.

"When I was little child, I'd go to this other reality, but I could never bring it back with me. I'm into my spiritual life most of the time. I get my touch; Thank God for this touch for giving me a safe place. I can feel the energy. There's energy all around us. Just stretch out your hand, concentrate on it, and you can feel it.

Worldwide it's happening; people are being taught how to feel the energy and use it to heal. In my class, I call it 'reconstruction.'

"In the morning, if you're feeling off, bathe yourself up and down with this energy and heal yourself. That's what the world is made of—this energy—and it brings peace of mind. So I don't think there's any 'inner' or 'outer' when it comes to spiritual life. It's all one. I feel the energy coming over me, and it affects my whole body like an overarching presence. At the bottom of all this, I believe there's a God, a Creator—bigger than we can conceive in our mind. All we have to do is get in touch with that. Everything is perfect; we just need to realize that."

When Barack Obama won the Presidency in 2008, Emerson described his first reaction—to heal the afflicted relationship he'd had with his father. He had been terrified of his father. A sharecropper and Baptist minister, his father had preached about love but never showed it. His life as a sharecropper had been unbearably brutal, driven by hardship, poverty, and abuse.

Emerson was only twelve when his mother asked him to watch over his father, then seriously ill, while she was at work. Just days before he died, Emerson overheard one of his father's final prayers, asking God to take care of Emerson because he knew he would not live to see him grow up. "I wanted so much to come in and hug him and tell him how much I loved him. But I was always afraid of him." He couldn't bring himself to make that final gesture.

All those years later, the seemingly impossible had happened: an African American had been elected President of the United States. Emerson, a gifted healer, though he wouldn't claim that for himself, explains why he reached out to his long-deceased father:

> Compelled by my memories of him and his suffering and mine, I have decided to write my father a letter, not that I expect him to read it or send me a letter in return. I feel an importance I've never felt before, as well as the consciousness

to speak beyond the veil that separates my father and me as I share this news with him. I feel it is my duty to do so.

The letter begins: (about half of the letter is excerpted here)

Dear Pappa,

This is your youngest son, Emerson. I am now eighty-five years old. I have fathered seven children. One died and I have six living.... My nine grandchildren have given me twelve great grandchildren. I think I did well carrying the Stamps name into the future.

But Pappa, I'm really writing you about the changes that have happened in my lifetime since you have left this reality. I never thought I would live to see the day when a Black person would be elected President of the United States of America. It has happened, and my pride in my country is only equal to that which I felt when I landed on Omaha Beach on June 6, 1944 and helped drive Hitler's army out of France to free the world of fascism. We unloaded guns and supplies, followed the Eighth Army all the way into Bonn, Germany. Then when I got back home and I went to the court house to get my discharge papers verified, and I still had on my uniform, the judge made me give up my seat to a white person....

You remember how you taught us to get off the sidewalk if a white person was walking by us and never speak to a white person unless they spoke to us first. Always say "yes, Ma'am" and "no, Sir" when speaking to white people, never looking them in the eye. You remember, Pappa? When you taught me not to talk to white folks, I know that was to save my life, so I wouldn't get hurt, wouldn't get put in jail. They'd hang Black people in trees. I remember a neighbor's son got shot for no infraction at all.

Well, that's all changed now, Pappa, through the efforts of many strong Black women and men who marched in the streets, attacked by dogs and club-whipped by police. Change rode in on the shoulders and deaths of those brave souls....

Pappa, I wanted to attend the inauguration in Washington, but the price of hotels was out of my range. There were buses, but you'd have to sleep on the bus and return the next day. I watched the inauguration on TV and I shared it with a friend who came from Mississippi and I cried with every word. Oh, Pappa, I forgot to mention the President is half white. You know in the South, if you were one-eighth Black, you were considered Black.

After the swearing-in, he gave his first speech as President. In my mind, he spoke for all those whose shoulders he stood on to get there, the river of tears and blood they waded through for this day. At the first of ten inaugural balls, he and his wife Michelle danced to the song "At Last." That was the same song my deceased wife and I chose as our wedding song. Again I cried....

I'm worried about his safety, knowing my country's history of what happens to a very popular president. Before he was elected, I told my friends he would need divine intervention to become president. So I pray the power that brought him into the office continues to sustain him throughout his presidency.

Love, Emerson

A beloved friend, Emerson holds a unique place in my constellation of friends. Now a wise elder, he's an inspiration for how to age with grace and humor. Yet what stands out above all is his unshakable faith in his life's purpose—that he came here to love, not only his family, but everyone. That is the quiet gift he is constantly giving, and it includes the invisible realms that are as accessible to him as anything in ordinary reality, something he speaks about with easy assurance. I love listening to his stories, such a welcome stretch for my rational mind! Wherever he goes, Emerson's presence is quietly healing. For me and for countless others, he is an *anam cara*, the beautiful, Celtic word for a beloved spiritual friend.

Photo courtesy of Olivia Hoblitzelle

STELLA FOX

THE GIFT OF RECOGNITION
STELLA FOX

S TELLA'S NAME MEANS "star." She stands next to her daughter Lorraine, the friend I'm visiting in Crestone, Colorado.
Lorraine's arm is resting protectively around her mother's shoulder. Stella, ninety-four, is a short, sturdy woman barely five feet
tall. She looks directly at me, the photographer. Her white hair
is pulled back from her round face with its broad nose, the folds
of age softening the strong lines of her chin and neck. She is
smiling, her eyes crinkled with delight at being included in the
photograph. From this moment caught on film, one would never
have guessed what sorrows lay in Stella's past.

Stella is a Blackfeet Indian. She grew up on reservations and in a
government boarding school for Indian children, one more forgotten victim of our oppression against Native Americans. Struggling
for an existence, she married one man after another—five in all—
each one bearing the hope that life might become better. She had
three children including Lorraine, and lost custody of them when
Lorraine was four years old. Lorraine had told me stories about
their family, the alcohol, the violence, and her mother's tragic life
with all its struggle, depression, and despair.

Throughout her adult life, Stella worked as a nurse's aide. She
started her career in Browning, Montana, where she was born,
and then left to work in Seattle and San Francisco. She had never
gone back because, as her daughter explained, she had experienced so much suffering in her early years, she chose to disasso-
ciate herself from her Indian roots.

The day I took the photograph was hot and dry. Lorraine's house sits on the arid plain where the majestic Sangre de Cristo mountains begin to rise steeply to 14,000 feet against the brilliant blue, cloudless sky. Now in her mid-nineties, Stella has come to live with Lorraine and her husband, and a new story begins to emerge.

June is the month of the Sundance, the annual, weeklong ceremonial gathering of the tribe for ritual, traditional dance, and shared community. Arduous as the trip and camping might be, Lorraine decides to bring Stella along so that she can see her old homeland. She hasn't been back to Montana, her homeland, for over fifty years.

On the last day of the Sundance, there is an elder-honoring ceremony. Because Stella is the oldest person at the encampment, the Sundance chief invites her into the center of the large circle to participate in the ceremony. She is introduced to the tribal leaders, who welcome her home. It is an overwhelming experience for Stella. Moved to tears, then weeping openly, many of those witnessing this moment are weeping along with her. They know something of her story. This is her welcome. This is her homecoming. This is honoring her as an elder in her tribe.

Then the Sundance chief gives Stella instructions for her part in representing all the elders who will be honored, and the ceremonies continue. For this day, she is at the center, participating in this ancient tradition in the most important ceremony of the year.

"In our tradition," explains Lorraine, "aging is a natural and noble process. Families are important and each individual is important, and above all, the elders are considered the repositories of wisdom. That is why they are honored at the Sundance ceremony. This was a life-transforming experience for my mother."

In the days and weeks that followed, instead of Stella's usual resigned, withdrawn expression, she began to shine, and the shining continued to the day of the photograph. As Lorraine saw it, some of her mother's lifelong wounding seemed to have been redeemed by the recognition and honor with which she was treated. She came out of hiding, out of the shadows of her suffering to stand proud at the center of that great gathering. As an old woman in a culture that honors its elders, she had been given the gift of recognition and respect.

A few years later, when Stella was in her late nineties and living in a Care Center in Alamosa in the San Luis Valley, Lorraine asked her if she wanted to live to be one-hundred. "She got this amused look in her eyes and said, 'Why not?'"

And she did. Her 100th birthday party was a front-page story in the Alamosa newspaper, with a photo of her sitting in her wheelchair as she received a blessing from her daughter. Four generations had gathered to honor her. One of the elders present said, "Stella is a real gift. Her friendship is a treasure. She's a wonderful lady."

When I asked about Stella's last years, Lorraine explained, "My mother always had a way of saying things in a simple and straightforward way and accepting whatever was happening to her. This survival mechanism served her well in facing the challenges of aging. It allowed her to live in the now, which is the challenge. She saw things as they were at that moment and didn't seem to hold on to things from her past.

"The nurses at the care center loved her. She was so grateful to be there because her life had been so hard. She used to reassure me, saying, 'Don't you worry about me. I have everything I need here. I'm OK right now.'

"And she was just fine, moment to moment. That got stronger as she became older. Even though she declined, and it sometimes seemed as though she was hardly there, there was always her presence. I feel as though presence—her presence—almost has form and weight. I certainly experienced that with her. She seemed to be shifting from form to formlessness, but there has to be acceptance for that to happen. That shift into formlessness is grace. Even though my mother's life was not always easy, she is at peace and full of forgiveness and grace. She is an example for us all."

I've never forgotten Stella or how inspired I felt by her story. We who are not part of an indigenous or Asian culture do not have rituals or ceremonies to honor our elders, nor any formal ways to mark the transition into the elder years. Not marking the major passages of the life cycle is a silent yet compelling omission. In contrast, when we hear Stella's story, we have a glimpse into the transformative power of a ritual that honors the elders.

Photo courtesy of Beth Howell

ALICE O. HOWELL

Living the Symbolic Life
Alice O. Howell

Effervescent. Merry. Expansive. Rollicking humor. Intellectual delight. Wise. Rainbow light refracting into bright colors.

These are the words that bubble up as I think about Alice, a friend of many years who has also been a guide, an inspiration, and loving elder. As I write this, Alice is in her ninetieth year, an ebullient and brilliant woman whose uniqueness can't be captured in words. To try to do so would be rather like trying to squeeze a large, exotic bird into a tiny cage.

I met Alice at the Transpersonal Psychology Conference in Bombay, India, in 1982, an extraordinary gathering of mystics, spiritual leaders, psychologists, and physicists—explorers of consciousness from East and West. Alice had been invited to offer a workshop on Astrology Through the Ages, her signature work on tracing the evolution of consciousness spanning tens of thousands of years.

Alice loves to tell you that as a young person she used to emphatically declare that astrology was "superstitious twaddle for nincompoops," allowing her to understand others' skepticism toward this ancient art/science. By any standards, she had an unusual and difficult childhood. Because of her father's work, she never experienced living in a family home; an only child, she and her parents lived only in hotels and never for more than three months at a time.

By the time she was eighteen, Alice had lived in thirty-seven countries and spoke four languages fluently. On the positive side, for someone so young, she had been exposed to an astonishing range of culture, literature, and history.

From the time she was four or five, she was already possessed by the search for meaning. Why am I here? What matters most in this life? Who am I? The eternal questions. By twenty-one, she still had not discovered the answers to her intense intellectual and spiritual longing.

"I was having a meltdown," she explains, "because I had studied endlessly for years but still felt that I had had no experience of God."

Then, on June 9, 1944, came the epiphany. Her father suggested that she see a man named Hermes (Marion Franz), a famous astrologer who had just read her father's astrological chart, for he too was in a difficult time. When Hermes drew up Alice's chart, he explained to her, "You have been looking for God, or spiritual understanding, all your life, and here are the patterns to validate that."[24]

In a matter of two hours, she writes in one of her books, her worldview turned upside down. Suddenly, after years of intellectual and spiritual searching, she saw the way open, and, specifically, how she could resolve the conflict between religion and science that had hounded her all through her childhood. Thus she was launched into her life's work.

On that same day, Hermes urged her to go downstairs to meet his teacher, one of the most eminent astrologers of that time, a remarkable man known only as "M." Alice describes him as a "hidden Master." M immediately saw Alice's thirst for both knowledge and spiritual experience and became her teacher of esoteric wisdom.

It was M who introduced Alice to a ritual for honoring Twelfth Night, a celebration from the esoteric traditions. It's a beautiful, moving way to start the year, to come together with others whose lives are also dedicated to service and to deepen that commitment. The heart of the ritual involves a ceremonial moment where each person, witnessed by the others, makes a silent commitment to their highest intentions for the coming year. This year was Alice's sixty-eighth honoring of Twelfth Night, a ceremony, she reminds us, replicated in small groups all over the planet, "forging another link in a golden chain that is reaching through the millennia."

Having started so young, now, by meeting these two remarkable teachers, Alice continued to build on what has become her astonishing knowledge of comparative religion, mythology, sacred geometry, classics, and history. She has had two primary passions: first, to plumb the depths of astrology and how it illuminates psychological processes. And second, how to discover the sacred in the commonplace as a way to inspire one's life.

As a serious student of Carl Jung for over thirty years, she was thrilled when she discovered that the Jungian archetypes matched the planets. She describes astrology as a symbolic language of archetypal processes. The chart is an *astronomical* map of the psyche which, when wisely read, can reveal the unique patterns of how a person processes experience.

Alice has a deep understanding of Jung and the spiritual dimensions of human experience. Eventually she was approached by an eminent Jungian analyst who asked if she would read his patients' charts—with their permission of course. This became the centerpiece of her work. Alice is now regarded as a pioneer in this field. Not surprisingly, her original work in this and related fields led to frequent invitations to speak at Jung Institutes across the U.S. and internationally.

All of us recognize when we're in the presence of someone who has mastered her field of knowledge. With Alice, her knowledge is so vast, it's awe-inspiring to be in the presence of her luminous yet playful intellect. She has a passion for words and their etymology. Storyteller, mythologist, and dream follower, she exudes a world of fun, ever at play in the fields of the intellect. She delights in making the invisible visible. It's as though she wears a cloak made of light, a diaphanous, iridescent material dancing in response to her delight, each moment revealing another mystery, another insight, another bit of wisdom.

She will as easily move from an apparently simple explanation of how to live symbolically to some profound explication of an astrological subtlety. Or she will make some astonishing statement such as, "The split between science and religion could be healed by a new cosmic science involving theoretical physics and a spirituality involving the esoteric mystical tradition of all the faiths who see an underlying unity."[25]

Ever committed to healing the split between science and religion or between the feminine and the masculine, she starts talking, for instance, about her devotion to the archetype of Hagia Sophia—holy wisdom, the feminine divine. She talks about the urgency of reclaiming the feminine principle, how the divine feminine was submerged by the patriarchy and male dominance of the Piscean Age.

For me, once a Christian disillusioned by its patriarchy and male-oriented language, I had my own epiphany when she explained how the early church fathers translated the word "spirit," previously always feminine as in *spirita sancta*, into its male form *spiritus sanctus*—thus dropping the feminine out of the trinity and just about everything else.

The sacred feminine had always been known as Hagia Sophia, she who co-created the world with God, as told in the book of *Genesis*, the masculine and feminine together bringing forth creation. Of course, how could it be otherwise!

Alice is the embodiment of Sophia energy—playful, scintillating, full of delight and creativity. Sophia—feminine energy—she explains, is to be found, both hidden and revealed, in the midst of ordinary life. She is ever on a quest to discover the sacred in the commonplace—another lifelong love, as she describes it. Pick up her wonderful book *The Dove and the Stone*[26] about Iona, the place of pilgrimage, a sacred island in the outer Hebrides of Scotland, and you will see her playful and profound way of viewing the world.

How to live the symbolic life—that is her invitation.

"It's clear that my job has been to find the sacred in the commonplace, because nothing in this world—nothing!—exists outside of "As above, so below." In other words, no object, whether in nature or made by human hands, can exist without an archetypal process at its core."

She would invite you to see delight and wonder in everyday objects, for every object can be seen at another level—as a process—she would explain.

"What physical thing makes one out of two going up and two out of one going down?" she asks mischievously. "It's an object used by many people the world over, an everyday object that we use without giving it a thought."

You struggle with possibilities, unable to provide an answer.

"A zipper!" she replies gleefully with a hearty chuckle.

"This ordinary object reveals the world of duality—the dichotomy of separation and unity that we live with mostly without noticing. Think about it, when you pull the zipper down, that separates the two sides of the cloth. When you pull it up—aha!—you unite the two opposites."

But that's not the whole story! The word "symbolus," using the Latin, means to unite, to put two things together that reveal a hidden meaning. Whereas the word "diabolus," means not only the devil but to pull apart, divide, separate.

She refers to her beloved Walter, and how he used to pull up his zipper when dressing in the morning, and declare emphatically, "Symbolos!" Then, undressing before bed, he would pull it down with the mischievous wink and declare, "Diabolus!"

She and Walter married in their sixties, a second marriage for both, as loving a relationship as you can imagine. She had had four children, raised them on her own, and is now a great-grandmother. Walter encouraged her to start writing, and what a waterfall of creativity ensued! Throughout her seventies and eighties, Alice has written eight books. Is that ever an inspiration for anyone determined to find passion in the later years.

Lest I underplay the extent of Alice's contribution to the fields of astrology and psychology, two of her books are on the subject, the most recent titled *The Heavens Declare: Astrological Ages and the Evolution of Consciousness.*[27] She traces how the evolution of our consciousness as a species through the great ages is reflected in the myths, symbols, and art of each age. Each age spans about 2,600 years—the Age of Cancer, the Age of Gemini, Taurus, Pisces, and finally now the Age of Aquarius—a work of encyclopedic knowledge that combines mythology, art, archaeology, history, and, of course, astrology.

Unlike anyone else I know, Alice's spiritual life is graced with a merry playfulness that is utterly disarming. Like a breath of fresh air, it dismantles the seriousness that characterizes many a religious tradition. One laughs a lot around Alice. One is bathed with her love of life, her revelations, and her delight.

Her merry outlook includes how she regards death. She tells a story about herself when she was seven years old. She discovered a dead bird and for three nights lay awake, terrified at the prospect that all living things should die. The next day, she went into her Grandma King's study, the most serious room in the house, closed the door, and spoke to God, saying "I will be as good as I can be, as best as possible, and serve You, but there is one thing You could do for me: Give me a happy death!" Stay tuned, she writes.

As someone who lives the symbolic life, dreams continue to be an important source of revelation for Alice. Many years ago, she told me about a landmark dream she'd had over thirty years earlier.

"I am saying good-bye to a dearly-loved older man in my life. Our hands are touching through a chain-link fence. I am in tears. Kindly, he says, 'Don't cry, my dear. We will meet again on Aberduffy Day.'

"I woke on a tear-wet pillow, and began to search for some Celtic festival I knew not of. I searched in vain. Then I thought of the Gaelic roots: *aber* means "river", and "duffy" comes from *dubh* which means black. Black river = Styx = death! So who wants to die when they can celebrate Aberduffy Day!" And Alice laughs heartily.

"I've never felt any fear of death since this dream," Alice explains, and indeed she talks about death as the next great adventure, and knowing Alice it probably will be.

MAUD MORGAN

THE SEARCH FOR FREEDOM
MAUD MORGAN

I WILL NEVER forget how I first met Maud. We spent our first
half hour together in silence, not the ordinary way to begin
an acquaintance but utterly memorable. We were both attending a Sensory Awareness workshop, one of those consciousness
expanding weekends characteristic of the humanistic psychology
movement in the '70s.

Much of workshop was conducted in silence. We'd been invited to pair off, and Maud and I were partners in an exercise yet
to be revealed. With a quick glance, I guessed that she was in
her seventies, a striking-looking woman with curly white hair,
angular features, and brilliant blue eyes. I sensed the presence of
a strong individual with a lot of energy.

One of us, the passive partner, was asked to lie on the carpeted
floor; the other, kneeling at her head, to be the active partner.
The exercise was very simple, yet profound. We were invited to
slowly, mindfully, place our hands under our partner's head, and
with utmost care and attention slowly lift their head a few inches
off the floor. The facilitator invited us to be deeply respectful
of this process, to feel the contours of the head, to be aware of
their energy, and above all not to let thoughts intrude into pure
experience. We were invited to open to the preciousness of this
one moment, where we had the privilege of cradling our partner's
head in our hands.

I became so immersed in the experience that the duality between my hands and Maud's head dissolved. Bathed in feelings

of tenderness and silent communion with this woman whom I didn't know, I never forgot Maud Morgan, the striking woman who had entrusted her head to me. What an unlikely statement!

Years later, when she must have been in her late eighties, Maud Morgan called me. "Olivia, it turns out that we're in the African drumming class together. Because of my vision, I can no longer drive at night, and I wonder if you could drive me to the class."

We had only snippets of time together, the fifteen minutes it took to get to and from the class. Even though I had had the intimate experience of holding Maud's head, I knew nothing about her personally. We slipped quickly into friendship and gradually pieces of her life emerged. Some I remember vividly from our night rides to and from our drumming class; others are from the memoir that she started at age ninety-two entitled *Maud's Journey: a Life from Art*. The first sentence of her memoir is thoroughly arresting:

"Toward the end of childhood I wanted to be a saint; at a certain point in midlife I wanted to be a whore; in old age I simply want to be myself. In spite of the help, or hindrance, of five psychiatrists, I only achieved this happy state in recent years (in her nineties)."[28] Her lifetime of exploring identities culminated in this one simple statement: "In old age I simply want to be myself."

Over a lifetime dedicated to art, she had become celebrated for her work. She was one of the artists who helped to usher in abstract expressionism. She was a bold, experimental pioneer whose works appeared in shows with well-known artists like Jackson Pollack, Robert Motherwell, Mark Rothko, and others. As she described it, "I was fortunate enough to be one of those right in the eye of the whole extraordinary force" of abstract expressionism.[29] Eventually her works ended up in a number of major museums across the country—the Museum of Fine Arts in Boston, the Metropolitan Museum of Art, and the Whitney, to name a few.

Her real birth as a painter happened in Paris in 1927, a time when a remarkable assortment of gifted writers and artists convened in that vibrant post-war period. She hung out at bistros with such celebrated people as James Joyce, Alexander Calder, and Ernest Hemingway. Maud became very good friends with Hemingway, who was one of the first people to give her feedback on her painting and understood the vision that inspired her abstract work, radical for those times. She and her new husband Pat also spent time with the Hemingways in Key West, including an extended fishing trip with Hemingway that provided him a rash of marvelous stories.

"What a wonderful era it was to be young and to be in Paris! It felt like the center of the world," she wrote. Her time there laid the foundation for her career as an artist, "toward accepting the necessity of art in my life and toward recognizing the difficulty of sustaining that work no matter what the circumstances."[30]

Maud was immersed in the vibrant, highly creative artistic scene of Paris of that time, but her career was far from easy. She had married Pat, a fellow artist, but he was jealous of her talent and found ways to undermine her confidence. Like many talented women, she struggled to balance a marriage, two children, and her art. It was a complicated marriage, and she felt she had abdicated her wild, free, independent self. "I needed to be loved for the maverick I was. Pat didn't want growth or change, which were my goals. He sensed danger in me."[31]

Maud's story is inspiring not only for her fierce dedication to her art but also for her determination to win back the freedom that her marriage had stifled. After being separated from Pat for twenty years, at age seventy-five she decided to divorce him. It was always mystifying to her how Pat had been able to exert such a negative psychological influence on her. She went into nine years of Jungian analysis in her seventies, something that surprised even her but helped her to take the final step of divorce "that gave me something deeper, a liberty of my soul."[32]

And what a life Maud led! She moved among the most celebrated artists of her time and was considered one of them. She had numerous shows of her work, including three shows from work in her '90s. "Painting was my blood stream," she once wrote. "I have always painted from the inside out. I become a hollow reed, a vehicle through which something passes."[33] Her work is bold, evocative, mysterious, and highly individualistic. One critic wrote that the forms in Maud's paintings, "created in masterful light and mobility, belong to a cosmic confrontation. You seem to have visioned our point in this universe in a cosmic experience, giving us a viable sense of our whirling world, of the depth of sun, sea and earth...."[34]

Writing about another of her pieces, a huge triptych, Maud explains her purpose in creating the piece. "When open, I wanted the triptych to have the effect of a religious apotheosis devoid of religious symbols or recognizable personalities. I wanted it to express pure elation, ... and I felt wonderfully gratified that (the owner) had understood the religious power of the piece exactly as I had hoped."[35]

Maud traveled extensively throughout her life. Two highpoints stand out in her narrative. As a young person, she had been absorbed reading about Gandhi and inspired "by his religious fervor, dedication and power, ... his believing in non-violence as a religious way of life, and the glorious dedication that was his life."

Some years later, Maud traveled to India with her mother to attend the National Congress. After the speeches, they had a chance to meet Gandhi. He invited them to follow him to his private tent. Amid the overwhelming crowds, volunteers created a square consisting of bamboo poles to protect Gandhi, his assistant, Maud, and her mother as he strode rapidly ahead. They were almost lost in the vast, seething sea of humanity that pressed against the poles while the crowd chanted his name with reverence and fervor. "I recognized it as the most intensely religious moment of my life,"[36] she wrote.

Among Maud's travel adventures, a second story stands out for how a terrifying situation led her to an extraordinary shift of consciousness. She was alone in Italy when she was attacked and robbed. Besides being physically injured, she lost everything important to her.

> An amazing thing happened. As I stood there, totally alone, I had a moment of ecstasy, a true epiphany. For the first time in my life I experienced the thrilling reality of belonging completely to humankind. I saw myself as a creature in proper proportion to the eternal, an infinitesimal speck but part of the whole. I was an isolated old woman in a strange country... but something new had happened, something greater than anything I had ever experienced, which completely changed my sense of reality. I was not alone. I was a strand in the fiber of life, a tiny component in the grand plan of the universe of the spheres, I was ecstatic and elated, feeling lighter than air, uplifted, to a different level.[37]

Glimpses into Maud's spiritual orientation appear here and there through her memoir. She describes her love of the little chapel high on the hills behind the house on their land in Canada. Stone by stone, she and her family built it, and it became a place where she went for sanctuary. After a moving encounter between her and a heifer, which she believed had come to comfort her in her sadness that day, she describes the event "as a beautiful affirmation of the oneness of the universe, all of us together, people, animals, plants, air and rocks. ... My sense of God, the supreme spirit, has always been, and still is, strong. It has involved me from time to time in one or another of the myriad structures created for worship."[38]

Perhaps the most extraordinary of Maud's travel adventures began when she was seventy-seven. She set off alone on a six-month trip to Africa. Her friends cautioned her, afraid she might die on the trip. She realized the difficulties and risks but had felt called by Africa for over forty years. "I felt young, strong, virginal and free. I was deeply involved in starting a new phase of life."[39] The Africa trip, which took her to fourteen countries, was "one of the best moves I ever made in my life." Her writing about it is deeply moving and evocative. This was an extraordinary adventure for a woman of her years, traveling alone. It was to open whole new dimensions in her life and her art.

> Wherever you go you feel the mystery of Africa. Why should I, a single, old, white woman feel so completely at home there where every other face is black? Why did they accept my presence without question? I cannot answer the 'whys' of Africa. … Its secret is deeper than skin, deeper than custom, deeper than history. When I was there, I was at home and very conscious of being a part of the human race. Africa inspires generic love.[40]

Woven through Maud's story is the search for freedom, a deep impulse that inspired her art, her relationships, and her entire life. One of the chapter headings in her memoir quotes Teilhard de Chardin, the French mystic, priest, poet, and philosopher: "The world is filled and filled with the Absolute—to see this is to be free."

The theme of freedom shines forth through much of her adult life, and again as she writes about her old age.

> I think the later period in a woman's life is one of the very best. … I gained a whole new sense of freedom. I began building up the emotional energy which allowed me to make an entirely new life in a new place, living alone and doing new work that was closer to my real feelings.[41]

In her memoir, Maud Morgan wanted to show the juggling of one woman's attempt at balancing a life of wife/mother/artist as well as sharing "the old-age happiness I am presently experiencing in the hopes that it will be catching." She ends her memoir with these last words, a wonderful epitaph for her life:

Age is a time of passion. ... Maybe later I will start to worry about death and dying, but I haven't quite finished living enough yet to forfeit my spare time to apprehension.

I do not ask how many more summers I will have like this. I am serenely happy. It is easier to reach this (nirvana/freedom) when you're older, easier to live in the present. No need to think much about the future. It's too short to bother with, and about the past you can think any way you want since most people who might check up on you have died. So why not give yourself up to the here and now? Genesis eternal.[42]

Maud died in 1999 at the age of ninety-six. She had led an exceptionally creative life. She'd been a celebrated innovator in the world of modern art, a mentor for many artists, a woman who lived life passionately until the end. She had an infectious *joie de vivre* that touched the lives of all who knew her. For me, from our first meeting at the workshop, through our brief friendship, and then getting to know her through her memoir, she is, among the bountiful gifts of her life, a model for how to grow old with exuberance, how to seek new experience, and how to embrace life fully—this one precious life we're given.

Photo courtesy of Nigelle de Visme

FATHER BEDE GRIFFITHS

OVERWHELMED BY LOVE
FATHER BEDE GRIFFITHS

L ET ME INVITE you to visualize a tall, slender man in his
eighties walking barefoot along a sandy path by the banks of
the Cauvery River in south India. The path weaves through a forest grove with glimpses of the river appearing here and there. He
walks with a gentle sense of purpose, shoulders slightly rounded
with age, his head bowed with attention to the path. His white
hair is long around his shoulders, his beard white. He is dressed
in the saffron cotton of an Indian *sannyasi* or swami, the soft
folds falling around his feet. Although he looks very much an
Old Testament prophet, in truth he's far ahead of his time in living and teaching about interfaith spirituality, more like a prophet
for our times.

This was Father Bede Griffiths. At the age of eighty-six, referring to a life-changing experience he'd had two years earlier,
he made the astonishing statement, "In the last two years, I've
grown more than in the previous eighty-four."

Before describing what lay behind this statement, I need to
provide a little background. Father Bede, born in England and
educated at Oxford, ordained as a Benedictine monk. In his late
forties, he was given permission to travel to India "to find the
other half of my soul," as he used to say. This was extraordinary for the early 1950s. In the midst of his monastic years in
the Benedictine monastery, he began exploring Eastern spiritual
traditions, immersing himself in writings from the Hindu, Buddhist, Sufi, and Taoist traditions. He was particularly drawn to

Indian philosophy, writing that it realized "the supreme achievement of the human mind ... in its quest of a true conception of God."[43] Against the prevailing forces within Western monasticism of that time, he finally got permission to help in the foundation of monastic life in India.

He settled at an ashram called Shantivanam, "Forest of Peace," in the province of Tamil Nadu in south India. Eventually he ordained as a sannaysi in the Hindu tradition. Starting with his passionate search for truth that led to exploring Eastern traditions, a major part of his life work was dedicated to integrating the wisdom of East and West. He wrote voluminously on the subject, published a number of books, and taught worldwide mainly in the last years of his life. With a simple yet vivid gesture, Father Bede would use his hand to illustrate the unity underlying the great religions. He would point to each of his fingers as representing a major tradition—Christianity, Hinduism, Buddhism, Judaism, Taoism, etc.—and then tracing with his fingers down to the palm, he would explain that if you go deep enough in any spiritual tradition, you find the mystical unity that underlies them all, his palm representing the unity that underlies the diversity.

To convey something of Father Bede Griffith's presence, he has been described as having "the intellect of a sage and the sweetness and candor of a child."[44] He possessed extraordinary equilibrium, a brilliant yet delicate intellect, lucidity, and humor. As someone said, "...to walk into Father Bede's presence was like hitting a clear wall of stillness. His quietness and stillness was all pervading. It was impossible to rush round him. ... One immediately quieted and wanted to do nothing but sit still in his presence."[45]

Hob and I met Father Bede at the same Transpersonal Psychology Conference in Bombay where we met Alice Howell. Struck by the combination of his gentle, loving nature and his gift for talking about complex spiritual issues, Hob traveled several times to Shantivanam to spend time in retreat with Father

Bede, whom he considered his primary teacher. Hob and he had both had classical educations, and they'd sit on the porch of his hut and share their love of poetry and literature, and explore spiritual questions together.

When Father Bede came to U.S. in 1991, twice he spent extended time in our family house in Vermont in what became an experiment in spiritual community. Russill and Asha Paul, his beloved and closest devotees, and Brother Wayne Teasdale created a daily schedule of prayer, meditation, study, and work, which combined elements of the Benedictine order with life at Shantivanam. Four times a day, they would gather in the meditation room for worship accompanied by the sublime music of Russill on his unitar, an instrument like a sitar that he had made himself.

Besides the gift of spending time with Father Bede around the edges of his two retreats at our house, I was inspired by the way he lived with total humility and simplicity. To give an example, in December of that year, there was a blizzard in Vermont. It was their first retreat, and they lost electricity: for three days, no heat, no water, and no light except for candles. The house was freezing. The four of them gathered around the fireplace, Father Bede stirring buckets of snow for drinking and cooking water, and all huddled on the floor to sleep in front of the fire. For a man in his eighties, frail with a serious heart condition, this was a heroic example of how to deal with adversity.

Now, in your imagination, return to Shantivanan and visualize Father Bede's hut where he lived for twenty-five years. With a roof thatched with palm leaves, his hut had only one room with a small veranda, where he would often sit reading or meditating. Early one morning, while meditating, suddenly, without any warning, a momentous episode began. "A terrific force came from the left and hit me on the head like a sledge hammer. It was very scary, and I thought I was going to die. I got ready, said the prayers, but then the inspiration came, 'Surrender to the Mother. Surrender to the Mother.'"[46]

He explained that it wasn't just his traditional devotion to Mary, but the feminine in all her forms—Earth Mother, Mother of God, the Black Madonna, his own mother, the Mother in all of Nature, and in motherhood itself. In her, he also saw the Shakti, the feminine divine energy, worshipped in the Hindu tradition.

"I feel it was this power which struck me. She is cruel and destructive (her Kali form), but also deeply loving, nourishing and protecting."

After the initial blow and loss of consciousness, Father Bede began to experience overwhelming love. Waves of love began to flow into him, and he called out to the person attending him, "I am being overwhelmed by love."

Later, when reflecting on the enormity of what had happened, he explained, "Death, the Mother, the Void—all was love. It was an overwhelming love, so strong that I could not contain myself. ... I knew 'I' had to die, but whether it would be in this world or another, I did not know. ... It was the 'unconditional love' of which I had often spoken, utterly mysterious, beyond words."[47]

According to the medical diagnosis, he'd experienced congestive heart failure, pulmonary edema, and a mild stroke. For several days, his life hung in the balance. He didn't speak for a week. A loving group of devotees gathered around him to provide around-the-clock care.

Although a life-threatening illness, slowly he began to improve and regain his strength. Some months after the episode, he was talking with a friend about his experience. Sitting in the shade of his veranda on a wooden chaise lounge, the sun beyond illuminated his slender, elderly body. Vines on the veranda framed his head and moved gently in the wind as he began reflecting on what had happened.

It seemed clear that besides the severity of the episode on the physical level, Father Bede had had a mystical experience. As always, he sought to understand the deepest levels of what had happened. A process seemed to have been unleashed. His reflections were astonishing and revelatory.

Psychologically, he explained later, "it was a breakthrough to the feminine." All his life, he'd been "fairly patriarchal and masculine, dominated by the left brain and the intellect, but the whole rational system had been knocked down and the intuitive, sympathetic world opened."

Now, he explained, he was living far more in his heart than his head.

"I feel the spirit coming down from the head to the heart, descending into the body, to the belly or the *hara*, to the second chakra, through all of the chakras to the *muladhara*, the root chakra. I'm rediscovering the whole sexual dimension of life now that it's opening itself up.

"The Mother is gradually revealing Herself. It's a continual process, bewildering at times, an inner transformation. Through meditation, it sorts itself out. Let the order come out of the chaos. The confusions of life are integral to the understanding, for God is not simply in the intelligible world, but God is the chaos, God is in the darkness, God is in the Mother. The chaos is *in* God.

"My rational mind is bewildered sometimes, but my body knows much more than my mind. My body has opened itself up to the deeper mind beyond the mind, guided by the spirit within which is integrating the whole process. The whole order of the universe comes out of that chaos.

"Enlightenment is the union of this divine reality with the chaos of nature, life, and matter in the world. You're on a journey and the horizon is there."

His hands, moving gently as if in a dance with his words, gestured how we are being led toward that horizon—the possibility of enlightenment. Always the teacher, always the seeker, he continued to expound on the ramifications of his experience.

"I got this sense of *advaita* (non-dualism), everything flowing into everything else. It's all One. All the diversities are contained in the One. And it's gone on ever since. I never feel separated from the earth, from people, from the trees, and yet the differences remain. Advaita tends to minimize the (multiplicities in the) universe, but the divine reality is present in everything, in everybody."

Going back and forth between describing what happened and interpreting what it meant to him, Father Bede felt that two images summarize the whole experience for him: the Black Madonna and Christ crucified. He went on to talk about the experience of darkness, an inevitable phase of the spiritual journey.

"You must go through the sense of darkness, the total emptiness, the total annihilation. You have to be ready to die, ready to let go. Jesus had to go through the darkness, feel forsaken, lose his God, because we have to let go of all our projections. Beyond the mind is the darkness of love; the way of love is in the darkness. Jesus becomes total love, because he totally surrendered. ... He is present in time and space and present *beyond* time and space. The whole universe is present in that mystical, spiritual body, the mystical body of Christ, Jesus in his transcendent state."[48]

Father Bede's experience—physical and mystical—was about love. As he described it, "Death, the Mother, the Void, all was love. It was an overwhelming love, so strong that I could not contain myself."[49]

Again returning to Advaita as a philosophical framework for his experience of love and non-duality, he said, "Advaita is an insight which transcends logic; it is beyond all dualities of every kind. The rational mind is limited by dualistic thought and is within those limits, but Advaita is an insight beyond reason and logic; it is pure awareness, pure light. ... I am trying to point to an experience which transcends thought. I feel it is this experience of Advaita with all its paradox which we have to seek as the very goal of life."[50]

In the months that followed this episode and a milder one that followed a month later, Father Bede brought both his intellect and spiritual understanding to explain the enormity of what had happened. He explained that in the first episode the Mother "struck" him and wounded him, while in the second episode the Mother overwhelmed him with love, and healed him.

The process went on for months, and he saw it in three levels: On the physical level, it was a stroke; on the psychological level, it was "a death of the mind"—a breakdown of the left-brain, rational mind and an awakening to the feminine intuitive mind; on the spiritual level, he spoke about Advaita—a transcendence of all limitations and an awakening to the non-dual reality.

I have returned to Father Bede's words over and over again, both written and in videos, to soak up the clarity and wisdom revealed from these two experiences and all that they revealed to him. Unlike most accounts of near-death experiences that stop at the level of description, Father Bede, given the depth of his knowledge, placed his experience within the context of the great religions. Yet this wasn't dry or intellectual; listening to him, I could feel the intimacy and power of his experience, and feel drawn in and embraced by his gentle passion. In the generosity of his sharing, he invited all of us into the possibility of experiencing what he had gone through: the balancing of the feminine and masculine within the psyche, the Oneness of all reality, and, finally, a great and boundless love.

I love that he saw the psychological and the spiritual as inseparable, that he drew brilliant connections between Advaita and Christianity, that he was open to the exploration of the new consciousness and how these were all interconnected. He saw, for example, that the collective unconscious is that ground from which we all emerge when we're born, before we develop our individual personalities, and how we all carry, subliminally, the memory of this ideal state where we were one. As he explains, "Our growth in body, soul and spirit is in some sense a return to this original unity... The Holy Spirit, Christ in us, pierces through every level of our being and makes us one in this ultimate ground. This is how everything and everyone comes out of unity and returns to unity."[51]

His immense physical suffering allowed him to share as never before in the suffering of Jesus on the cross, and along with that, the suffering of the world. And woven through it all was a powerful love that he felt within himself, the gift of the feminine combined with his lifelong dedication to a life of the spirit. "Nothing could stand in the way of that love—least of all death. I feel that death is only its ultimate embrace."

A lifelong contemplative and exceptionally wise teacher, Father Bede was also mystic. Fully aware that most people are not drawn to explore the mystical dimensions of life, he thought everyone should realize that this knowledge is accessible through spiritual practice, especially meditation. The transcendent mystery is available to all. As he once said, "The supreme is present among us and we must be aware that at every moment and in every place, we are in the presence of that divine mystery."[52]

In his last days, those caring for him reported that he spoke only of love. Love had become his entire universe and the core of his consciousness. He told Russill, his closest disciple who was with him until the end, "I feel that God has created a love and understanding in us that I have never experienced before and that has completed my life. It is a plan of total love, of total self giving love." In his dying days, he would often say, "I am so happy, I am so full of love."

In those last days and at his funeral, Russill played the Purusadic hymn that Father Bede had loved with "a passion that was overwhelming."[53] It's the only way to end this brief profile of a holy man.

> I know that great Person
> of the brightness of the Sun
> beyond the darkness.
> Only by knowing him
> one goes beyond death.
> There is no other way to go.

Conclusion

I T WAS A simple phrase mentioned in passing. My friend Helen was leaving to visit her mother, who was showing signs of early dementia, as yet undiagnosed. "She's in uncharted territory," said my friend. "My sister and I—we're all in uncharted territory."

The phrase "uncharted territory" stayed with me, a fitting description for the unknown realms of the late years and our efforts to live those years as consciously and wisely as we can. As I intuited the feelings behind Helen's words, I was reminded of those many instances when Hob's unraveling mind left us both trying to fathom the mysteries of dementia—sometimes lost, always searching. Understanding Alzheimer's and support for caregivers were still relatively new fields, and I would feel overwhelmed each time I encountered his latest loss, unexpected behavior, or confused effort to communicate. I would think about the countless others who were dealing with similar situations, equally challenged, and lost in the uncharted territory of aging and dementia. We're all in this together, so how do we get through?

The impetus to write *Aging with Wisdom* arose in part from the challenges of having both my mother and Hob ravaged by Alzheimer's, but my feelings go far beyond my own circumstances. Aging in an age-phobic culture is challenging. We need guidance and roadmaps. I've had my antennae out for years, looking and feeling my way. *Aging with Wisdom* offers highlights along this journey, the fruits of that search, propelled by my passion to pass along what I have found helpful, even lifesaving.

Every guide wants to make sure their fellow travelers have received the most important coordinates for reading the map. Surprisingly, several key guidelines appeared through the agency of a dream. We can listen to the messages of our dreams, especially landmark dreams that offer powerful, archetypal images that address our issues, known and unknown. As I was completing *Aging with Wisdom*, I had a dream that bears an uncanny relationship to the subjects that I had been writing about.

I am with several others traveling in an unfamiliar place. I am writing about spiritual practice, formulating guidelines for a process I am in. Carefully, I outline each letter in luminous, metallic silver ink, highlighting every word. Later, I reopen the book to make sure the highlighting is still there.

Meanwhile, we're playing a game that involves placing sticks in the ground. In the middle of the game, I begin to dissolve. My ordinary consciousness is thinning out, and I think I am transitioning—or dying. My friends are watching me closely with keen interest. I have absolute trust in the process I am experiencing.

I say to them, "Since I'm going, it's better to keep things simple."

From here, there is the sense of fewer words, fewer boundaries—a sure sense that I'm dissolving into emptiness—dying.

I woke up elated. Feeling the impact of these powerful images, I tried to remain in the dream state—dissolving into emptiness, dying, and the freedom that accompanied it. Even though I was dying in the dream, I felt absolute trust in what I was experiencing—the process of dissolving, this major transition in consciousness from life into death, the greatest transition of all.

"Since I'm going, it's better to keep things simple" is a striking statement and the only words spoken in the dream. These words point to the ultimate level of reality where dying can be simple. On the physical level, dying simply happens from one breath to the next. At the same time, of course it can be complex and harrowing. As in the dream, all of us are in different stages of dissolution. If we live with awareness, soften the ego's tendency to grasp, and practice letting go throughout our life, we are preparing ourselves for the final letting go into death. Again in reference to the ultimate level of reality, some traditions regard the moment of death as offering the possibility of liberation, the ultimate freedom.

The other dream image—outlining the text with silver ink—suggests that words about spiritual practice deserve deepest respect. They have been rendered sacred by the numinous. The silver ink transforms the ordinary into the sacred.

Let me highlight some of the signposts recounted in *Aging with Wisdom* that can provide inspiration for our elder years. You might look upon these as the most important guidelines and seed thoughts for further reflection.

- Rejoicing in the blessings we still have
- Letting go of our struggle with life
- Acceptance of loss and change
- Seeing beauty in old age
- Cultivating lightness and humor
- Deepening awareness through meditation
- Opening to the unknown
- Making friends with death
- Cultivating the life of the spirit

An overarching theme of *Aging With Wisdom* is that the elder years invite us closer to the mysteries of life and the life of the spirit. Certainly the last part of my dream about the process of dissolution reveals how consciousness transitions from life into death and affirms trust in that process. It also alludes to an ultimate level of reality where spirit is all that remains, and freedom is spirit's ultimate gift. Throughout our lives, we seek that sense of freedom, whether consciously or not, and most especially in our elder years.

I'm reminded of the words of Paul in one of his letters to the *Corinthians*, "…though this outer person of ours may be falling into decay, the inner person is renewed day by day." The body and mind may decline in all manner of ways, culminating in a final illness, but the spirit is indestructible. This is both solace and inspiration.

In the words of philosopher George Santayana, "Nothing is inherently and invincibly young except spirit, and spirit can enter a human being perhaps better in the quiet of old age and dwell there more undisturbed than in the turmoil of adventure."[54] Our ultimate refuge is in deepening our inner life and cultivating the life of the spirit. I know I could not have handled the challenges of my loved ones' dementia and dying without the companionship of meditation practice.

To grow old is in the natural order of things. That too is beautiful, despite the stark reality that old age, sickness, and death can be brutal and unforgiving. Beauty and pain exist, side by side. Can we stay open to both? We must; for that is the challenge life asks of us.

It was remarkable that my friend Mary, much loved in the large community she was a part of, wanted to share her dying process openly, to let it be a teaching for all who chose to be with her.

Mary was dying. A contemplative by nature, she had led a full, creative life, an artist whose great talent sought to convey the mysteries of the inner realms. She knew she was dying. Instead of narrowing the circle of people around her, as many people understandably do, she said that she wanted to share her dying; she wanted her family and friends to see that dying was a natural process and that there was nothing to fear.

Every evening a small group of us gathered around her bed for meditation. From week to week, she weakened. Her body became thinner and frailer. Her words were few, but her eyes became ever brighter—a shining blue—calm, radiating a wordless depth. That she shared her dying days in this way was exceptional. Her gentle spirit eclipsed the ravages of the body and gave the gift of beauty to how she was living her last days. She died peacefully, surrounded by her loved ones. Her death was indeed a gift.

There can be many gifts in the realm of aging. It depends on our perspective, whether we have the wisdom to see beyond our personal story to the greater reality of which we are a part, to deepen our inner life and open to the mysteries of life and death.

In speaking of that mystery, the Sufi master asks, "Is this not a better path? Is this not a way that goes backward away from the body toward the light from whence you came?"[55] Finding the light of wisdom that guides us through our elder years, and the light into which we die, these illuminate both our living and our dying.

> Again, traveler, you have come a long way led by a star
> But the knowledge of the wish is at the other end of night,
> May you fare well, *companero*,
> Let us journey together joyfully,
> Living on catastrophe, eating pure light.[56]

Like the traveler in this epitaph, we've come a long way through life. What a wonderful wish that we might journey together joyfully, however our journeys unfold from here.

ENDNOTES

[1] Alice O. Howell, *Credo*. A series of essays appear on her blog. "Jung on Aging" http://ionadove.blogspot.com.

[2] Christian McEwen, *World Enough & Time: On Creativity and Slowing Down* (Peterborough, N.H.: Bauhan Publishing, 2011), 213.

[3] Claudia Hammond, *Time Warped: Unlocking the Mysteries of Time Perception*. As quoted in Wikipedia on Time Perception, excerpt quoted in *Changes with Aging*.

[4] Op. cit., McEwen, 313.

[5] David Whyte, "Enough," *Where Many Rivers Meet* (Langley, WA: Many Rivers Press, 1998), 2.

[6] "The Unbroken." © 1991 by Rashani Réa. www.rashani.com.

[7] John O'Donohue, *Anam Cara: A Book of Celtic Wisdom* (New York, NY: HarperCollins Publishers, Inc., 1997), 167.

[8] Shantideva, *The Way of the Bodhisattva*.

[9] Albert Einstein. As quoted in Eben Alexander, M.D., *Proof of Heaven: A Neurosurgeon's Journey into the Afterlife* (New York, NY: Simon & Schuster Paperbacks, 2012), 76.

[10] Trans. Anita Barrows & Joanna Macy, *Rilke's Book of Hours: Love Poems to God* (New York: Riverhead Books, 1996), 48.

[11] Coleman Barks with John Moyne, *The Essential Rumi* (New York, NY: Harper San Francisco, 1995), 36.

[12] William Blake, *The Marriage of Heaven and Hell* (London: Dover Publications Inc., 1994). Quoted on Wikipedia, "The Doors of Perception."

[13] Quoted in Larry Rosenberg, *Living in the Light of Death: On the Art of Being Truly Alive* (Boston, MA: Shambhala Publications, 2000), xii.

[14] Ibid.

[15] Robert Peter Tristram Coffin. Fragment from his poem "Crystal Moment." As Hob quoted it from memory, there is no page reference.

[16] Evelyn Ames, *The Hawk From Heaven* (New York, NY: Dodd Mead & Co., 1957), 60.

[17] Rainer Maria Rilke. Excerpt from a letter to Countess Margot-Sizzo-Noris-Crouy. Quoted in trans. Joanna Macy & Anita Barrows, *A Year with Rilke* (New York: Harper One, 1999), 6.

[18] Sherwin B. Nuland, *The Art of Aging: A Doctor's Prescription for Well-Being* (New York: Random House, 2007), 173. His Indian friend's translation of this quote.

[19] Quoted in Joseph Goldstein, *One Dharma: The Emerging Western Buddhism* (New York, NY: HarperCollins, 2002), 33.

[20] Henri Nouwen, *Life of the Beloved: Spiritual Living in a Secular World* (New York: The Crossroad Publishing Company, 1992), 110.

[21] Henri Nouwen, *Our Greatest Gift: A Meditation on Dying and Caring* (New York: Harper San Francisco, 1994), 42.

[22] Master Sheng Yen, "Remembering Sheng Yen." Quoted in *Tricycle: A Buddhist Quarterly*, Summer 2009, end page with photo.

[23] Emerson Stamps, *Don't Look Them in the Eye: Love, Life, and Jim Crow*. Boston, MA. Independently published, 2010.

[24] Kate Sholly, "The Heavens Declare: A Conversation with Alice O. Howell," *The Mountain Astrologer*, December 2009/January 2010, 27.

[25] Ibid. 28.

[26] Alice O. Howell. *The Dove in the Stone: Finding the Sacred in the Commonplace*. Wheaton, IL: Quest Books, 1998.

[27] Alice O. Howell, *The Heavens Declare: The Astrological Ages and the Evolution of Consciousness* (Wheaton, IL: Quest Books, 2006)

[28] Maud Morgan, *Maud's Journey: A Life from Art* (Berkeley, CA: New Earth Publications, 1995), 11.

[29] Ibid. 132.

[30] Ibid. 213.

[31] Ibid. 131.

[32] Ibid. 232.

[33] Ibid. 188.

[34] Ibid. 196.

[35] Ibid. 200-1.

[36] Ibid. 222.

[37] Ibid. 163.

[38] Ibid. 163.

[39] Ibid. 233.

[40] Ibid. 159.

[41] Ibid. 227-8.

[42] Ibid. 266-7.

[43] Shirley Du Boulay, *Beyond the Darkness: A Biography of Bede Griffiths* (New York, NY: Doubleday, 1998), 171.

[44] Ibid. 255.

[45] Ibid. 252.

[46] *Return of the Feminine*, a video. The following excerpts come from this video.

[47] Ibid.

[48] Ibid.

[49] Du Boulay, *Beyond the Darkness*, 230.

[50] Video excerpt.

[51] Ibid.

[52] Du Boulay, *Beyond the Darkness*, 254.

[53] Ibid. 263.

[54] George Santayana. Quoted in Harry Moody & David Carroll, *The Five Stages of the Soul: Charting the Spiritual Passages That Shape Our Lives* (New York: Doubleday, 1997), 155.

[55] Ibid. 156.

[56] Thomas McGrath. Epitaph quoted in Robert Bly, *American Poetry: Wildness and Domesticity* (New York: HarperCollins, 1990).

SELECTED BIBLIOGRAPHY

Albom, Mitch. *Tuesdays with Morrie*. New York: Broadway Books, 1997.

Alexander, Eben, MD. *Proof of Heaven: A Neurosurgeon's Journey into the Afterlife*. New York, NY: Simon & Schuster Paperbacks, 2012.

Ames, Evelyn. *The Hawk From Heaven*. New York, NY: Dodd Mead & Co., 1957.

Anyen Rinpoche. *Dying with Confidence: A Tibetan Buddhist Guide to Preparing for Death*. Boston: Wisdom Publications, 2010.

Barks, Coleman, with John Moyne. *The Essential Rumi*. New York, NY: HarperOne, 2004.

Bateson, Mary Catherine. *Composing a Further Life: The Age of Active Wisdom*, New York: Alfred A. Knopf, Inc., 2010.

Bauby, Jean-Dominique. *The Diving Bell and the Butterfly: A Memoir of Life in Death*, Paris: Editions Robert Laffont, S.A., 1997; New York: Alfred A. Knopf, Inc., 1997.

Bernhard, Toni. *How To Be Sick: A Buddhist-inspired Guide for the Chronically Ill and their Caregivers*. Somerville, MA: Wisdom Publications, 2010.

Blackman Sushila. *Graceful Exits: How Great Beings Die*. New York: Weatherhill, 1997.

Chittister, Joan. *The Gift of Years: Growing Older Gracefully*. Katonah, N.Y.: BlueBridge, 2010.

Church, Forrest. *Love & Death: My Journey Through the Valley of the Shadow*. Boston: Beacon Press, 2008.

Coberly, Margaret, *Sacred Passage: How to Provide Fearless, Compassionate Care for the Dying*. Boston, MA: Shambhala Publications, 2002.

Dalai Lama, His Holiness. *Advice on Dying and Living a Better Life*. New York: Atria Books, 2002.

_____. *The Mind of Clear Light: Advice on Living Well and Dying Consciously*. New York: Atria Books, 2003.

Dimidjian, Victoria Jean. *Journeying East: Conversations of Aging and Dying*. Berkeley, CA: Parallax Press, 2004.

Du Boulay, Shirley, *Beyond the Darkness: A Biography of Bede Griffiths*. New York, NY: Doubleday, 1998.

Erikson, Erik H., and Joan M., *The Life Cycle Completed*. New York, NY: Norton, 1997.

Feldman, Christina. *Compassion: Listening to the Cries of the World*. Berkeley, CA: Rodmell Press, 2005.

Fischer, Kathleen. *Winter Grace: Spirituality and Aging*. Nashville, TN: Upper Room Books, 1998.

Gawande, Atul. *Being Mortal: Medicine and What Matters in the End*. New York, N.Y.: Metropolitan Books, 2014.

Goldstein, Joseph. *One Dharma: The Emerging Western Buddhism*. New York, NY: HarperCollins, 2002.

Griffiths, Father Bede. *Discovering the Feminine*. Sydney, Australia, More Than Illusion Films, 1993.

Grollman, Earl A. and Kenneth S. Kosik, M.D. *When Someone You Love Has Alzheimer's*. Boston, MA: Beacon Press, 1996.

Gullette, Margaret Morganroth. *Agewise: Fighting the New Ageism in America*. Chicago: University of Chicago Press, 2011.

Halifax, Joan. *Being with Dying: Cultivating Compassion and Fearlessness in the Presence of Death.* Boston: Shambhala, 2008.

Heilbrun, Carolyn G. *The Last Gift of Time: Life Beyond Sixty.* New York: Ballantine Books, 1997.

Howell, Alice O. *The Dove and the Stone: Finding the Sacred in the Commonplace.* Wheaton, IL: Quest Books, 1998.

_____. *The Heavens Declare: Astrological Ages and the Evolution of Consciousness.* Wheaton, IL: Quest Books, 2006.

Kabat-Zinn, Jon. *Wherever You Go There You Are: Mindfulness Meditation in Everyday Life.* New York: Hyperion, 1994.

Kalanithi, Paul. *When Breath Becomes Air.* New York: Random House, 2016.

Kornfield, Jack. *A Path With Heart: A Guide Through the Perils and Promises of Spiritual Life.* New York: Bantam Books, 1993.

Luke, Helen. *Old Age: Journey Into Simplicity.* New York: Parabola Books, 1987.

McEwen, Christian. *World Enough & Time: On Creativity and Slowing Down.* Peterborough, N.H., Bauhan Publishing, 2011.

Moon, Susan. *This is Getting Old.* Boston: Shambhala, 2010.

Morgan, Maud. *Maud's Journey: A Life from Art.* Berkeley, CA: New Earth Publications, 1995.

Morrison, Mary C. *Let Evening Come: Reflections on Aging.* New York: Doubleday, 1998.

Morse, Melvin M.D., *Closer to the Light: Learning from the Near-Death Experiences of Children.* New York: Ivy Books, 1990.

Nouwen, Henri, and Walter Gaffney. *Aging: The Fulfillment of Life.* New York: Doubleday, 1974.

_____. *Our Greatest Gift: A Meditation on Dying and Caring.* HarperCollins: New York, 1994.

_____. *Life of the Beloved: Spiritual Living in a Secular World.* New York: The Crossroad Publishing Company, 1992.

Nuland, Sherwin B., *The Art of Aging: A Doctor's Prescription for Well-Being.* New York: Random House, 2007.

O'Donohue, John. *Anam Cara: A Book of Celtic Wisdom.* New York, NY: HarperCollins Publishers, Inc., 1997.

Pradervand, Pierre. *The Gentle Art of Blessing: A Simple Practice That Will Transform You and Your World.* New York: Atria Paperback, 2009.

Raines, Robert. *A Time to Live: 7 Tasks of Creative Aging.* New York: Penguin Books, 1998.

Richmond, Lewis. *Aging As a Spiritual Practice.* New York: Gotham Books, 2012.

Rilke. Translated by Anita Barrows & Joanna Macy. *Rilke's Book of Hours: Love Poems to God,* New York: Riverhead Books, 1996.

_____. *A Year with Rilke.* New York: HarperOne, 1999.

Ring, Kenneth. *Heading Toward Omega: In Search of the Meaning of the Near-Death Experience.* New York: Quill/William Morrow, 1984.

Rohr, Richard. *Falling Upward: A Spirituality for the Two Halves of Life.* San Francisco: Jossey-Bass, 2011.

Rosenberg, Larry. *Living in the Light of Death: On the Art of Being Truly Alive.* Boston: Shambhala, 2001.

Rumi, Jalaluddin. *The Essential Rumi.* Translated by Coleman Barks with John Moyne. New York: Harper San Francisco, 1995.

Schacter-Shalomi, Rabbi Zalman. *From Age-ing to Sage-ing.* New York: Warner Books, 1995.

Schwartz, Morrie. *Letting Go: Morrie's Reflections on Living While Dying.* New York: Walker & Co., 1996.

Scott-Maxwell, Florida. *The Measure of My Days*. New York: Knopf, 1968.

Shantideva. *The Way of the Bodhisattva*. (Bodhicaryavatara) Revised edition. Boston: Shambhala, 2008.

Singh, Kathleen Dowling. *The Grace in Dying: How We Are Transformed Spiritually as We Die*. New York: Harper SanFrancisco, 1998.

_____. *The Grace in Aging: Awaken as You Grow Older*. Somerville, MA: Wisdom Publications, 2014.

Smith, Huston. *Tales of Wonder: Adventures Chasing the Divine*. New York: HarperCollins, 2009.

Smith, Rodney. *Lessons from the Dying*. Somerville, MA: Wisdom Publications, 1998.

Sogyal Rinpoche. *The Tibetan Book of Living and Dying*. New York: HarperCollins, 1992, revised 2010.

Stamps, Emerson. *Don't Look Them in the Eye: Love, Life, and Jim Crow*. Boston, MA. Independently published, 2010.

Surya Das, Lama. *The Big Questions: How to Find Your Own Answers to Life's Essential Mysteries*. New York: Rodale, 2007.

Thomas, Dr. Bill. *Second Wind: Navigating the Passage to a Slower, Deeper, and More Connected Life*. New York: Simon & Schuster, 2014.

Tolle, Eckhart. *The Power of Now*. Novato, CA: New World Library, 1999.

Tulku Thondup. *Peaceful Death, Joyful Rebirth: A Tibetan Buddhist Guidebook*. Boston: Shambhala, 2005.

Whyte, David. *Where Many Rivers Meet*. Langley, WA: Many Rivers Press, 1998.

ABOUT THE AUTHOR

OLIVIA AMES HOBLITZELLE, a writer and teacher, was formerly the Associate Director of the Mind/Body Clinic and a Teaching Fellow of the Mind/Body Medical Institute, where she pioneered how to bring meditation, yoga, and cognitive behavioral therapy into the medical domain to treat stress-related and chronic illness. She and her team developed one of the first training programs in Mind/Body medicine in the country and trained health professionals under the auspices of Harvard Medical School.

Formerly a therapist in private practice and a Co-Director of Greenhouse, an alternative mental health collective, Olivia worked with individuals, couples, and groups. She also spent years serving as a Hospice volunteer.

Olivia's teaching and writing are inspired by over forty years of practice in psychology, Buddhist meditation, and other wisdom traditions. In addition to her roots in Christianity, she has practiced primarily Vipassana (Insight Meditation) and Tibetan Buddhism, as well as in a devotional tradition from India.

Having taught contemplative practices in a wide variety of settings such as government agencies, hospitals, churches, businesses, school systems, and meditation centers, she is currently focusing on conscious aging, elder issues, and living the contemplative life.

Her award-winning book, *Ten Thousand Joys & Ten Thousand Sorrows: A Couple's Journey Through Alzheimer's*, is a narrative memoir of how she and her husband handled his illness, drawing inspiration from their background in Buddhist practice.

Now an elder with two grown children and four grandsons, she lives in Massachusetts and loves to spend time in Vermont where she grows vegetables, welcomes family and friends, and steeps herself in the glories of nature.

Acknowledgments

ALL BOOKS UNFOLD in mysterious ways, as they are a tapestry of influences and interconnections. There are many threads in *Aging with Wisdom*: ancestors, friends, family, teachings, books, council circles, conversations, and many more. Undoubtedly, life itself has been the main inspiration.

For a journey that started almost fifty years ago, my deepest gratitude to all my dharma teachers, starting with Vipassana, evolving through a devotional tradition from India, to my Tibetan Buddhist teachers. Their inspiration and wisdom has influenced my life beyond measure.

With delight and deepest thanks, I acknowledge my immediate family, Ethan and Elise Hoblitzelle, Laura and Randy Bak, and my four grandsons. They provide more love and support than they will ever know.

As we've moved into the later years, my three siblings grow ever closer: loving thanks go to Oakes, Ned, and Joanie and their respective spouses Louise Ames and Jane Sokolow. Given the nature of this book, I want to express deep gratitude for our parents Amyas Ames and Evelyn Perkins Ames whose vivid, creative, and loving lives touched mine in countless ways. Because we spent so much formative time with grandparents—and two appear in the book—I would like to name them: my Danish grandmother Olga Flinck and Henry Perkins, Blanche Ames and Oakes Ames. A bow of gratitude to four remarkable people.

Heartfelt gratitude to my three longtime circles, each one a treasure of connection and wisdom: the Self-Ordination Circle—still meeting after eighteen years: Louise Cochran, Ilona O'Conner, Demaris Wehr, and Ann Dunlap; the Campers group with Ferris Urbanowsky Buck, Judith Abbott Laskaris, and Islene Runningdeer; and the Wednesday meditation group with Emerson Stamps, Donna Svrluga, Richard Griffin, Charles Busch, and my late husband Hob.

Given how the gifts of friendship inspire our lives, I want to acknowledge those who are connected to the evolution of the book: Jeff Scannell, Sam Black, Peter Forbes, Helen Whybrow, Robert Jonas, Margaret Bullit-Jonas, Linda Coe, Sam Fisk, Anne Nash, Joan Diver, Nigelle de Visme, Monique Pommier, Shannon Gilligan, Anne Burling, Penny Gill, Paula Green, Jim Perkins, Nyia Yannatos, Wendy Garling, and Debbie Roberts. Although no longer with us, their presence is very much in this book: Natalie Rogers, Alice Howell, Polly Starr, Ray Montgomery, Margot Wilkie, Emerson Stamps—beloved all.

Warm thanks to my agent Stephanie Tade with whom I loved working even though the book found its place via an unexpected route.

Although I have always hesitated to work professionally with friends, thank heavens I made an exception with dear friend and master editor Arnie Kotler. With his sensitivity and skill, he nudged me into further needed improvements, provided continuous support, and ultimately introduced me to Paul Cohen, my publisher. For earlier editing, thanks to Jeanne Braham.

It has been a joy to work with Paul Cohen, Publisher of Monkfish Book Publishing Company, who is dedicated to bringing out cutting edge, spiritually oriented books, and his associate Colin Rolfe who designed the book. Filled with wonder at all you do, my hearty thanks to you both.

To Margaret Harding, miracle worker, wizard, and saint, I'm not sure any amount of thanks will do the trick. She and I know how many rabbits she pulled out of that proverbial hat. Also Sarah Oinonen whose warmhearted presence and many skills helped in countless ways. Warmest thanks to Mary Greer; most of the book was written in an alcove in her house.

Barbara McCollough and I have been "task companions" for over twenty years—an exceptional relationship and marvel to us both. Her support, feedback, and love are measureless. Special thanks also go to Prajna Lisa Hallstrom, Demaris Wehr, and several others who read parts of the book at different stages and provided valuable feedback. For those whom I have forgotten to name, know that my appreciation is still there!

Finally, my partner Keith Taylor has been a stalwart and loving support throughout. I thank him for everything but above all for his boundless heart—the greatest gift of all.

READING GROUP GUIDE:
QUESTIONS FOR DISCUSSION
AND SELF-REFLECTION

Since *Aging with Wisdom* covers many subjects that invite further discussion, the following Reading Group Guide can serve as a framework for book groups. I have included a number and range of questions, so that participants can choose the most compelling ones for discussion.

PART I

- When you hear the phrase "conscious aging," what does it evoke for you? What would it mean to wake up to your life in new ways, to approach situations more consciously?

- Can you give examples of ageism you've experienced and discuss their impact? They can be very subtle. For example, a pejorative comment, condescending language, hostile jokes about aging, excluded from conversation, etc.

- What is your orientation toward the inner life? Do you have a spiritual practice of any kind, and if not, discuss how and where you find meaning in your life.

    We need to acknowledge that some people may not be comfortable with the word "spiritual." The central question is how you inspire yourself when faced with life's biggest challenges. Some people, for example, have a philosophy of life that includes cultivating positive qualities like compassion, kindness, generosity, equanimity, joy, love, and so on.

- As you've grown older, whether or not you've experienced a "tectonic shift," can you describe the ways in which you've recognized your growing older, and what, if any, changes you've made in your life—or would like to make.

- Carl Jung and other wise ones have called old age the most valuable period in life. Discuss how you feel about this statement, and whether it applies or not to your experience so far.

- What are the gifts of aging? In contrast, what are the challenges, disappointments, and harsh realities of aging?

- As we seek to balance the different elements of the aging process, what does the phrase "the grace of diminishment" mean to you? How do you relate to Teilhard de Chardin's statement about hallowing one's passivities and diminishments?

- Have you recognized your particular responses to the challenges of aging? Examples: resistance, denial, control mode, anger, fear, grief, etc.

- Almost inevitably, issues of independence and/or growing dependence arise in the later years. Some people find it really difficult to accept help, even reject help as a sign of weakness. What are your feelings about this subject?

- Whether or not you relate to the idea of a "forest monk" stage of life, has there been any shift toward deepening your inner life, toward reflection or contemplation of some kind?

- Have you noticed any impulse to simplify or downsize or change some of the outer circumstances of your life?

- The ElderSpirit credo offers exceptionally rich possibilities for discussion.

- Reflecting on the idea of "soul time" (that some cultures have very different views of time from ours), how is the quality of your life affected by time? Can you relate to the African porters who refused to go on because they were "waiting for their souls to catch up?"

- Consider the challenging words of Rashani's poem—brokenness, shatteredness, sorrow, fragility, darkness—and how you relate to these. How do we find "...the place inside that is unbreakable and whole/ While learning to sing?"

- In telling the story of the old man, discuss the Dalai Lama's statement that "there's no reason to feel old just because the body is old."

Part II

- "The sacred circle that shelters your life." Consider together what this might mean to you and share these reflections with the group.

- The idea of taking refuge is common to many spiritual traditions. What are your refuges?

- What if you tried "to treat every moment as new experience?" What areas of your life might change? Have you ever considered what it would be like to lose your sight, how much we take our senses for granted?

- In what ways do you connect with others through some practice of the heart, whether blessing, prayer, wishing them well, or simply calling them into presence with love?

- Who are you now? Has your sense of self shifted as you've aged, perhaps as you've moved away from a nine to five job, parenting responsibilities, and so on.

- Loss is a major issue for all of us as we age. (Physical problems, memory loss, diminished sight/hearing, loss of dear ones, etc.) What are your thoughts/feelings about the issue of loss. How does your inner life help?

- We receive many memorable messages during our lives. What two or three have had a powerful impact over your life?

Part III

- The story of Dhumavati challenges many of our assumptions, such as a goddess archetype that describes many cruel aspects of old age. How do you feel about this story?

- The subject of death presents us with the ultimate koan—a paradox or riddle, unanswerable by the rational mind. What have been your experiences with death and dying, and what feelings arise for you as the group turns to this discussion?

- In the various excerpts about death (Rilke, Tagore, Thoreau, Nouwen, Master Sheng Yen), what do you find thought provoking, inspiring, or challenging?

- Mysterious occurrences may occur around or after death. Have you experienced or heard any stories that speak to this mystery?

- The Five Remembrances, or similar calls to remember the subject of death, are considered important practices in several spiritual traditions. How do these sayings strike you?

- We are seeing an epidemic of dementia-related diseases like Alzheimer's. Have you been close to someone with dementia and if so, what has that brought up for you?

- If one accepts that there is consciousness beyond the mind, how might this affect how one relates to someone with dementia, particularly in the later stages?

- What are your feelings when you hear someone say that death is a gift?

Part IV

- As you reflect on this term "wayshower," who have been wayshowers for you? What inspires you about them?

- Each of the six wayshowers in this section reveals something unique about their elder years. Can you name some of those unique qualities and what stands out about that wayshower?

- Is there one wayshower with whom you particularly identify?

- In the Conclusion, return to the list of the book's important guidelines and see which ones are most compelling for you. Some may provide a springboard for further discussion.

- What is the most valuable message that you've taken from your reading of *Aging with Wisdom*?